MALCOLM TORRY

# 101 REASONS FOR A CITIZEN'S INCOME

Arguments for giving everyone some money

POLICY PRESS SHORTS INSIGHTS

First published in Great Britain in 2015 by

Policy Press
University of Bristol
1-9 Old Park Hill
Bristol
BS2 8BB
UK
t: +44 (0)117 954 5940
pp-info@bristol.ac.uk
www.policypress.co.uk

North America office:
Policy Press
c/o The University of Chicago Press
1427 East 60th Street
Chicago, IL 60637, USA
t: +1 773 702 7700
f: +1 773 702 9756
sales@press.uchicago.edu
www.press.uchicago.edu

© Policy Press 2015

British Library Cataloguing in Publication Data
A catalogue record for this book is available from the British Library.

Library of Congress Cataloging-in-Publication Data
A catalog record for this book has been requested.

ISBN 978-1-4473-2612-0 (paperback)
ISBN 978-1-4473-2614-4 (ePub)
ISBN 978-1-4473-2615-1 (Mobi)

Cover design by Andrew Corbett
Front cover: image kindly supplied by Getty
Printed and bound in Great Britain by CMP, Poole
Policy Press uses environmentally responsible print partners

# Contents

## B   A CHANGING SOCIETY

## C   ADMINISTRATION

# CONTENTS

## D POLITICS

## E IDEAS

# Acknowledgements

I continue to be enormously grateful to all those who have stimulated my interest in the UK's benefits system, and in a Citizen's Income as a feasible and desirable way of reforming it. I will not repeat here the list of names to be found in the acknowledgements at the beginning of *Money for Everyone*, except to say that in the context of this present book I continue to be most grateful to the trustees of the Citizen's Income Trust with whom I continue to work happily as honorary Director; to the Social Policy Department at the London School of Economics, and particularly to Professor Hartley Dean, for appointing me to a second period as a Senior Visiting Fellow from 2013 to 2015; to Emily Watt and her colleagues at the Policy Press for their help and encouragement; and to Professor Jay Ginn for reading a draft of this book with considerable diligence, and for offering suggestions that were both detailed and helpful. Needless to say, any mistakes are entirely the author's responsibility.

All royalties from this book will be donated to the Citizen's Income Trust.

# Preface

It might seem strange to suggest that we should give to every citizen a sum of money every week, but this book offers a hundred and one good reasons for doing it.

The regular weekly income for which I offer so many reasons goes by a variety of names – Citizen's Income, Basic Income, Citizen's Basic Income, Universal Basic Income. They all mean the same thing: an unconditional and non-withdrawable income paid automatically to every individual as a right of citizenship.

By 'unconditional' we mean that the amount of Citizen's Income that someone receives would not be affected by employment status, by other income, by household structure, by gender, by marital status, or by anything else. The amount of Citizen's Income would vary with the age of the recipient – with children receiving less than working age adults, and older people more – but every individual of the same age would receive exactly the same amount every week.

By 'non-withdrawable' we mean that if someone began to earn an income, or their earned or other income rose, then their Citizen's Income would not change.

Here I must add a note about the term 'Citizen's Income scheme'. A Citizen's Income is an unconditional and non-withdrawable income for every individual. That definition never alters, and if an income does not fit that definition then it is not a Citizen's Income. A 'Citizen's Income scheme' is a Citizen's Income, along with the age thresholds chosen and the amounts of Citizen's Income for each age group, and also the changes made to tax and benefits systems when the Citizen's Income is implemented. There will therefore be numerous different kinds of Citizen's Income scheme.

At least since Thomas Paine wrote his *Agrarian Justice* the idea of a Citizen's Income has appeared about once a generation and then fallen back into obscurity. In 1984, following an increase in interest in the Citizen's

Income idea in a variety of European countries, a group of people came together to form the Basic Income Research Group in order to promote debate on the idea of a Citizen's Income so that it would not disappear from view and there would be a more solid basis for discussion when it re-emerged. The Europe-wide and now global organisation Basic Income Earth Network (BIEN) soon followed. The Basic Income Research Group is now the Citizen's Income Trust, and now that we are a generation from 1984 we are pleased to see the expected renewed interested in Citizen's Income schemes. In the UK the Green Party has recommitted itself to establishing a Citizen's Income; we have seen increasing interest in the press and social media; and a variety of campaigning groups have emerged. Elsewhere, Namibia and India have experienced successful pilot projects, Switzerland is soon to hold a referendum on whether the country should establish a Citizen's Income, and academic and policy-maker interest is evident around the world.

Because a Citizen's Income would positively serve our economy and society in a variety of ways, and because our current benefits system is no longer appropriate to our society or to its economy, we need to grasp this moment of opportunity to promote widespread debate about the desirability and feasibility of a Citizen's Income – and then to implement it.

It is for this reason that I wrote *Money for Everyone: Why we need a Citizen's Income*, and that the Policy Press published it in 2013. *Money for Everyone* is a thorough, evidence-based discussion of the desirability and feasibility of a Citizen's Income, and it serves well as an introduction to the subject. The book is both accessible and academically rigorous, but some of those who have read it have asked whether I might write a further book – shorter, even more accessible in style, and suitable for stimulating initial interest in the subject. This is that new book.

In the cause of accessibility and brevity I have kept notes and references to a minimum. Anyone who wishes to pursue a particular argument, or to discover the evidence for it, should easily find relevant material by using the comprehensive indexes in *Money for Everyone*. Only where a quotation needs to be referenced, or where no reference to a source will be found in *Money for Everyone*, will an endnote be found. No index is provided because the detailed contents page will take the reader to passages relevant to their interests. Because the book might be used in this way I have tried to ensure that each reason is self-contained: that is, readers will not need to refer to other parts of the book in order to understand the reason that they are reading. Because the same logic, or the same evidence, might underlie more than one reason for a Citizen's Income, the reader who reads the book all the way through will notice a certain amount of repetition. Take, for instance, the marginal deduction rate: the total rate at which income taxes and withdrawal of means-tested benefits reduces disposable income as earnings rise (the deduction rate is 'marginal' in the sense that it is the rate at which *additional* earnings are reduced). If a Citizen's Income were to replace all or most of current means-tested benefits then the marginal deduction rates for many households would be lower. This would have a variety of different effects, which is why a Citizen's Income's ability to reduce marginal deduction rates appears in the descriptions of a number of different reasons for a Citizen's Income. Similarly, a reason for a Citizen's Income might encapsulate several other separate reasons already discussed, so previously discussed reasons will be summarised in order to argue for the reason in question. I hope that anyone reading the book all the way through will not be too put off by the repetition necessitated by my attempt to ensure that each of the many different reasons is self-contained.

Why a hundred and one reasons? Because when I wrote a list of reasons for implementing a Citizen's Income, I ended up with well over a hundred. This was going to produce too long a book, so I reduced the number to a hundred and one.

The reasons for a Citizen's Income are divided into five categories: the economy, a changing society, administration, politics, and ideas; but as I wrote the book I found it more difficult to categorise than I had expected. Quite a lot of them could easily have gone into more than one category, so the categories to which some of the reasons have been allocated are necessarily somewhat arbitrary.

The book is designed for an international readership, and most of the text of each reason for a Citizen's Income will be immediately accessible to anyone from any context. I use general terms wherever possible (so 'means-tested benefits' rather than the specifically UK 'Jobseeker's Allowance' or 'Working Tax Credits'). However, it is important to show how the effects of a Citizen's Income would compare in practice with the effects of today's benefits systems, and because the current tax and benefits systems of different countries can be very different from each other, we can find ourselves comparing a Citizen's Income with a wide diversity of different systems. As the systems of tax and benefits in the United Kingdom of Great Britain and Northern Ireland are the systems that I know best, when I want to show in practice how the effects of a Citizen's Income would differ from those of a current system I take the UK's system as a case study. Aspects of the current systems in other countries get an occasional mention, but there is no way in which a book of this length can offer a comprehensive treatment relating to so many different systems around the world. An important justification for taking the UK as a detailed case study is that its benefits system contains means-tested, social insurance, and universal benefits, and its tax system includes both social insurance contributions and a progressive income tax.

It therefore contains in essence the building blocks out of which most of the world's benefits systems are built. It should always be clear from the text whether I have tax and benefits systems in general in view or whether I am writing specifically about the UK. To help the reader in this respect I have capitalised the names of UK benefits, but not the more general description of benefits. So 'means-tested benefits' is a description of any benefit anywhere in the world the calculation of which takes into account the claimant's other income, whereas Jobseeker's Allowance is the UK benefit that might be either 'contributory' – that is, a social insurance benefit – or 'income related' – that is, means tested. Readers not from the UK should be able to translate the UK case study into their own context fairly easily, and the note on the UK system that follows this preface should assist in this process.

*Money for Everyone* was designed as both a set of distinct arguments for a Citizen's Income and as a single cumulative argument. This book is the same. Whether the arguments that I offer for a Citizen's Income are persuasive is up to the reader to judge, and equally the reader must judge whether I have adequately answered the objections to a Citizen's Income that I list near the end – but the fact that there are *so* many reasons for making this change in the way in which we administer tax and benefits systems does rather suggest that it is time we seriously considered making that change.

*Malcolm Torry*
*London*
*February 2015*

# The constituents of benefits and tax systems, and the UK as an example

(The proper names of UK benefits and taxes will be capitalised. So, for instance, 'income tax' means any country's tax on income, whereas 'Income Tax' means the UK's Income Tax.)

Developed countries' benefits systems tend to be made up of three elements: means-tested benefits, social insurance benefits, and universal benefits.

A means-tested benefit can be either an 'out-of-work' benefit, given to an adult of working age who is not in employment because they cannot find work, they have onerous caring responsibilities, or they are sick or disabled, or an 'in-work' benefit, given to an adult of working age who is in employment but whose wages are regarded as insufficient to maintain a decent standard of living. Means-tested benefits are normally allocated to benefit units containing more than one individual rather than to individuals, and because much of the literature employs the term 'household' for the benefit unit, I shall do so too, even though the benefit unit is not always strictly a household. The amount of means-tested benefit that a household receives depends on the amounts of other income coming into the household and on the household's financial assets. (A means test is a combination of an income test and a savings test.) The higher the other income, the lower the benefit. UK examples of out-of-work means-tested benefits are Income-based Jobseeker's Allowance and Incapacity Benefit, and Working Tax Credits are an example of in-work means-tested benefits. Housing Benefit and Council Tax Support (a rebate applied to a local property tax) can be paid both in work and out of work. The new Universal Credit, which is slowly being rolled out across the UK, is a combination of all of the main means-tested benefits.

A social insurance benefit is paid out on the basis of contributions paid in by someone who is employed and by their employer, or by someone who is self-employed. Usually, the longer the contribution record, or the more money that has been paid into the fund, the higher the benefit. In some countries social insurance benefits are managed by the State, but industry, employer, and trade union schemes also exist. Benefits are paid out when a relevant contingency applies, such as unemployment or sickness. Benefits are generally time limited, but they are usually not means tested. UK examples of social insurance benefits are the Basic State Pension and Contribution-based Jobseeker's Allowance. (If unemployment continues beyond six months then the means-tested Income-based Jobseeker's Allowance is paid instead.) The reader will discover that the UK's 'National Insurance' contributions and benefits bear little relation to insurance premiums and benefits.

A universal benefit is paid to people in a particular age group without a means test and without contribution conditions having to be satisfied. A UK example is Child Benefit which, following a residency test, is paid for every child living in the UK. A different amount is received for the first child of each family than for the second and subsequent children, but the same amount is paid for every first child, whatever their parents' income or wealth, and similarly for every second and subsequent child.

Most tax systems are based on a progressive income tax. Each individual or household is allocated a personal (or household) tax allowance, and earnings up to the allowance are not taxed. Beyond the allowance, earned and other income is taxed, often with different rates applied to different income levels. So someone earning a high income will usually not be taxed up to their tax allowance, then on the next band of income they will be charged a low rate, and then on subsequent bands the rates will rise. The UK example is Income Tax which operates in this way and is applied to each individual and not to households.

Social insurance contributions will often be levied alongside income tax, either by the State or by an industry body, an employer, or a trade union. In the UK, National Insurance Contributions are paid to the State alongside Income Tax. Up to an initial threshold no contributions are collected. After this point they are collected at 12% of earnings (but not on other income) up to an Upper Earnings Limit, and beyond that point they are collected at 2% of earnings. The system is therefore not progressive – that is, the rate of contribution falls rather than rises as earnings increase.

Developing countries might exhibit some of the characteristics of the systems that have evolved in developed countries, but not necessarily all of them.

# A
# THE ECONOMY

# 1

# A Citizen's Income is easy to describe

I make no apology for repeating here what I have written in the preface, because before reading the rest of this book it is essential to grasp what a Citizen's Income is.

A Citizen's Income is an unconditional and non-withdrawable income paid to every individual as a right of citizenship.

By 'unconditional' we mean that the amount of Citizen's Income that someone receives would not be affected by employment status, other income, wealth, household structure, gender, marital status, or anything else. The amount of the Citizen's Income would vary with the age of the recipient – with children receiving less than working age adults, and older people more – but every individual of the same age would receive exactly the same amount every week.

By 'non-withdrawable' we mean that if someone began to earn an income, or their earned or other income rose, then their Citizen's Income would not change.

It really is as simple as that: a payment to every individual, every week, with everyone of the same age receiving exactly the same amount, whatever their circumstances.

Some people call this a 'Basic Income', or a 'Universal Basic Income', and some of us call it a 'Citizen's Income'. Whichever term we use it is an unconditional and non-withdrawable income paid automatically to every individual.

It might be helpful to be clear what would *not* be a Citizen's Income. A benefit that goes down if wages or other kinds of income rise is not a Citizen's Income; a benefit that is reduced if someone has savings is not a Citizen's Income; a benefit that is paid to a household rather than to an individual is not a Citizen's Income; a benefit that requires the recipient to look for a job, or to have a caring role, or to fulfil any other condition of whatever kind, is not a Citizen's Income.

If a nation state were to pay a Citizen's Income then a citizenship or residency test would of course be required to determine who should receive it; but if any other kind of test were to be used then it would cease to be a Citizen's Income (an interesting question is whether prisoners should receive Citizen's Incomes). If a continent-wide Citizen's Income were to be implemented, then a citizenship or residency test relating to that continent would be required. But again, no other test would be permitted.

A Citizen's Income is an unconditional and non-withdrawable income paid automatically to every individual as a right of citizenship. It's as simple as that.

# 4

# A Citizen's Income would provide security during changing employment patterns

My grandfather worked for the same engineering company from one end of his working life to the other, and that was normal. Today, employees will often experience several changes of employer, of occupation, and of employment status: periods of self-employment, full-time employment, part-time employment, unemployment, study, caring for relatives, and often a mixture of two or three of these at the same time. This diversity can offer variety of experience, and it can enable us to develop different skills, but we shall only benefit from change if we have secure parts of our lives that do not all change at the same time. There is little more stressful than moving to a new place and a new job, with perhaps one's partner giving up his or her job in the process, and then being made redundant – but this is not an uncommon experience.

A Citizen's Income would alleviate some of the effects of frequent change by providing a secure income as our employments change, and it would give to everyone a greater ability to make their own positive choices in the employment market.

During the 1970s some negative income tax (NIT) experiments took place in the United States. A NIT is not a Citizen's Income. With NIT, earned income above the tax threshold is taxed, and if earnings fall below the tax threshold then the tax system pays out a benefit. But because the disposable income effects of a NIT and a Citizen's Income are similar, results from the experiments can tell us how a Citizen's Income might affect behaviour. Researchers found that most of the small employment reduction effect of a NIT was people between employments taking longer to look for their next job. [2] This is a good thing. It is better to have the financial security to be able to seek the job that best suits our skills, residential location, and caring responsibilities, than to be forced by poverty or benefits rules to accept any job that is offered.

A Citizen's Income would cushion us from some of the worst effects of a more flexible labour market; it would give to us the flexibility to seek the right job at the right time; and, because it would enable more people to refuse insecure jobs, it might also encourage employers to offer better jobs.

# 5

# A Citizen's Income would tackle the precarity trap

While I was growing up my father left for work at the same time every day and he returned home at the same time every day. He did occasionally get a new job, with a new public sector employer, but always in the same field – housing management. He entered employment when he left school and he exited it when he retired.

Life can now be very different, and we have witnessed new and, to us, unfamiliar employment patterns among our own children – casual labour, home working, zero-hours contracts (that is, working when the employer requires work, but not otherwise), short-term contracts, low-paying self-employment – and often two or more of these employment types at the same time. And then there are the unpaid internships that have become the only gateway to too many occupations. 'Work for labour' – that is, work to find employment – is ubiquitous, and no longer can people expect to belong to a profession or a consistent occupation, so too many miss out on the satisfactions that such belonging can offer.

This is the experience of the 'precariat': a new and growing class that can include any of us. For someone without employment, entering employment that might last a few weeks and then exiting again can mean multiple changes to benefits claims, which is a reason not to enter precarious employment in the first place. And taking on commitments – to a home, to a partner, or to children – in a situation in which both employment and benefits are precarious, can look daunting. And for someone in apparently secure full-time employment suddenly to find themselves in the precariat can be devastating.

In countries in which the provision of healthcare is an employment benefit, and one not attached to zero-hours, casual, or short-term employment, members of the precariat can find themselves dangerously without healthcare. The UK is fortunate in its unconditional National Health Service – an important factor in enabling the UK to weather the trend towards greater precarity. The same logic would apply to financial provision. An unconditional and non-withdrawable income would provide in the financial sphere the same kind of security that the NHS provides in healthcare.

Precarity is not going to go away. Our now global labour market will ensure that. A Citizen's Income – an income that would never change as employments and self-employments came and went – is the only viable financial basis for security in the midst of such precarity. [3]

# 6

## A Citizen's Income could make zero-hours contracts useful

The employment market is becoming more flexible – but is this a good thing?

It sometimes is as far as the employer is concerned. In a restaurant in which the number of customers varies from day to day, it can be efficient for the employer to employ people when demand is high, and not to employ them otherwise. So 'zero-hours' contracts – which pay people to work when required to do so, but otherwise do not – can be efficient for the employer.

Provided that such contracts are not restrictive – that is, as long as they enable the employee to decline to work a shift if it is offered at short notice, and as long as they do not prevent someone from accepting other employment – they can also be efficient for the employee, particularly if they are a student or they have varying caring responsibilities. The only problem with such contracts is the varying wages that they pay: a problem compounded by the current benefits system. The calculation of means-tested benefits – whether in-work benefits or out-of-work benefits – takes into account the level of earnings. Where successive calculations are designed to be rare events, and to set a benefit level for a lengthy period, it can be difficult to decide precisely what to count as someone's wage level if their pay changes rapidly. Where calculations are undertaken monthly (as with the UK's new Universal Credit) keeping up with changing earnings from a variety of sources can be impossible.

The only solution is to abandon such calculations and to pay a Citizen's Income. This would provide an income floor on which people could build a variety of zero-hours contracts and other earnings. They would never again have to declare their earnings to an administrator, and never again would an administrator wonder how to calculate the correct amount of benefit.

At the time of writing, there is talk of prohibiting zero-hours contracts. Some employees would regret the end of a type of contract that suits them. Zero-hours contracts need to be non-restrictive, and they need to come with better employment conditions, but abolition is neither necessary nor sensible.

For most of us, full-time secure employment will remain the norm, and there are reasons for thinking that a Citizen's Income would make it more common; but for some people, for some of the time, zero-hours contracts can be useful. To turn them into a positive experience, all that is required is the financial security that a Citizen's Income would help to achieve.

7

# A Citizen's Income would make part-time employment worthwhile

The 'main breadwinner' in a family is generally employed full time, and the 'secondary breadwinner' either full time or part time. Alternatively, neither partner is employed, because if the main breadwinner is on means-tested benefits then their partner generally gives up their employment because most of the amount of their wages is deducted from the family's benefits.

Most jobs therefore have to be full time, and most part-time jobs have to offer a sufficient number of hours, and sufficient pay, to enable employees to benefit financially. This all makes for an inflexible labour market because it means that industry and commerce have to provide large numbers of full-time jobs, even when full-time jobs might not be the best way to organise things. It also makes it difficult for many parents to spend enough time with their children, or with other people for whom they are caring.

The labour market *is* slowly becoming more flexible, despite such problems. There are now more people employed part time, often in job shares, and self-employment is becoming more popular, and these changes are occurring in spite of a tax and benefits system that discourages part-time employment and self-employment. But what we do not see much of is part-time earning among main breadwinners, be they men or women.

Many couples would prefer both to be employed part time (which might mean two or three full-time days), or for the sole breadwinner to be employed part time, something difficult to achieve at present unless the part-time earnings are substantial. And what many families would like to see end is the nonsense whereby means-testing makes almost worthless the earnings of the partner of someone who is unemployed and on means-tested benefits.

A Citizen's Income would give to every family and to every individual an income floor below which they could not fall, and because their Citizen's Incomes would not be withdrawn as earnings rose, it would encourage greater flexibility in employment patterns. Somebody unemployed would be more able to take part-time employment or to create self-employment; one partner could be unemployed without the earnings of the other becoming worthless; and two parents could both be employed part time so that both could spend more time with their children.

If we had a Citizen's Income, then part-time and/ or short-term employment would be easier for more people to accept, and because individuals would have greater choice as to what they could accept, the labour market would become a free market and would be more efficient in providing people with the employment that they wanted and industry with the labour that it needed.

8

# A Citizen's Income would reduce unemployment

Unemployment is a draining experience. A job provides social contact, a role, escape from too much close family contact, an income, a sense of achievement, the ability to provide for oneself and for a family, the fulfilment of our need to work, partial escape from the guilt imposed by a work ethic rooted in religion and social pressure, and a way of exercising responsibility. To lose a job is to lose all of that, and possibly one's home as well. For anyone on means-tested unemployment benefits, most of a spouse's earnings are deducted from benefits income and one unemployed person in a family can therefore become two. It is not surprising that redundancy and unemployment are demoralising experiences. There are now about two million officially unemployed people in the UK. [4] The social damage, in terms of ill health and family breakdown, is enormous.

By creating more opportunities for people to earn their way out of poverty through self-employment or part-time employment, a Citizen's Income would reduce the number of those who wanted paid work and could find none which they could accept; it would provide continuity between employment and unemployment, thus minimising the sense of disruption; it would express social belonging and would thus lessen the isolation felt during unemployment; and by inviting people to re-enter the employment market in a variety of ways (unlike out-of-work means-tested benefits, which disincentivise employment and prescribe labour market re-entry methods) it would reduce the frustration felt by people who go for job after job and are not even invited for interview.

Unemployment will continue to be a draining experience. To have held a full-time, fulfilling job and to lose it will always be traumatic; but because a Citizen's Income would offer continuity during transitions, create a variety of ways out of unemployment, and make a statement about the person's continuing membership of society, it would reduce the importance of the category 'unemployed'. There would still be people who wanted employment and would not be able to find it – for instance, residents of a town in which a major employer closes down – but fewer people would be classified as 'unemployed' because many of those now in this category will have used their Citizen's Income as a springboard out of the unemployment trap and into new economic activity.

## 9

# A Citizen's Income would correct wage levels

What would happen to wages if tax allowances and much of our current benefits system were to be replaced by a Citizen's Income? Would the employee's increased financial security mean that employers would be able to pay lower wages? Or would increasing financial security enable people to decline to work for low wages and thus cause wages to rise in order to attract people into jobs?

In the UK, different means-tested benefits are paid in and out of work, so benefits do not constitute the kind of financial security that would generate upward pressure on wages; and in a variety of countries work tests and sanctions mean that governments force people into employment without wages having to rise to attract them. Means-tested in-work benefits are calculated after employees know their wage levels, so the employee will generally not know how much benefit they will receive. The wage subsidy effect will therefore be low and somewhat unpredictable.

For 'good jobs', with good working conditions, satisfying social networks, and inherently interesting work, wages might fall. People want these jobs because they provide self-esteem and other advantages, so the existence of the Citizen's Income might mean that an employer would not have to pay as much to attract applicants as they do now. For 'lousy jobs', with poor working conditions, and with tasks not inherently interesting, a secure Citizen's Income might mean that the employer would have to increase the wage offered in order to attract applicants, and might have to improve working conditions.

Because we all have different preferences – for money, leisure time, inherently valuable work, etc. – we would expect a Citizen's Income to have different effects for different people. For some people, including some in 'good jobs', their Citizen's Income might provide them with the opportunity to leave employment or to reduce their hours of employment, so wages might have to rise to attract employees. Some people would prefer to keep their 'lousy jobs' – for a variety of social and other reasons – so their employers might not have to raise their wages to keep them. The aggregate outcomes are somewhat unpredictable, so one possibility would be to pay a Citizen's Income to one age group to start with, watch the effects, and then move on to the next age group. However, it is probably reasonable to assume that, in the aggregate, wages would rise for lousy jobs and fall for good jobs. This seems entirely right. It is how markets are supposed to work.

# 10

## A Citizen's Income would compensate for low wages

In the 1950s, the south bank of the Thames was a string of labour-intensive industries: electricity generation, docks, warehousing, and heavy engineering. Workforces were full time and well paid, mainly because they were sufficiently large to make effective organisation possible and a strike meant immediate loss of profit.

Those businesses are now either highly automated or they have been attracted abroad by lower wage costs, and large public sector workforces are being broken up by the contracting out of services to multinational companies. Even in the car industry, strikes have little effect because production can continue in other countries; and because a strike is as likely to result in a factory's closure as in a wage rise, strikes have become few and far between. Except where employees have a monopoly, and production cannot be moved abroad (underground train drivers are a good example), downward pressure on wages will be inexorable. National Minimum Wage rates are always set low enough to avoid any suggestion that unemployment might rise because of them, and the result is declining disposable incomes, reductions in in-work benefits in order to control the government's budget, and people working longer hours in order to make ends meet (in spite of the European Working Directive's attempt to cap working hours).

In a context of falling wages, and of defensive minimum wage legislation, in-work benefits will remain an important means of maintaining household incomes. But in the UK, apart from Child Benefit, in-work benefits are means tested, which means that any increase in earnings will only substantially benefit employees who are not on in-work benefits. Because wage supplements are means tested, the less the employer pays, the more the employee receives from the State. Declining wages therefore cost all of us increasing amounts of money. A Citizen's Income would not rise as wages fell, so it would act as a static subsidy and not as a dynamic one. It would therefore have less of a depressing effect on wages.

We need a benefits system that would enable households to increase their disposable incomes more rapidly than they can now, and which would provide a completely secure income floor that would blunt the effect of falling wage levels at the same time as encouraging the search for new opportunities for higher earnings. Our current benefits system cannot achieve this, whereas a Citizen's Income would enable people to weather more easily the frequent changes in employment patterns and earnings levels that an increasingly global labour market will bring.

# 11

# A Citizen's Income would improve employment incentives

Remarkably, even though employees on low wages receive little financial benefit from employment because they lose so much money through benefits withdrawal, they still wish to be employed – but the fact that taking a part-time or low-paid job will generate little additional disposable income is still a disincentive. The evidence for this is the job-search requirements and sanctions attached to means-tested out-of-work benefits. There is not much carrot, so a stick is used. If there was always a sizeable financial incentive to seek employment then no longer would the stick be needed. Compulsory job-search and the sanctions attached to it indicate system failure. What is required is not more sanctions, but a better system.

Some people find it hard to accept the idea of a Citizen's Income that would 'pay people for doing nothing'. Would a Citizen's Income not destroy a work ethic that is already under threat? Would it not stop people from seeking employment? Would it not mean that essential tasks ceased to be carried out?

There would be two opposing effects. On the one hand, cutting the number of hours of employment would be a financial possibility, and, on the other, additional employment would generate more disposable income than it would now. With a high Citizen's Income the former pressure might be the stronger, but with any realistic level of Citizen's Income, the latter would determine the outcome – particularly as good employment provides a variety of additional advantages, such as self-esteem and social networks.

A Citizen's Income would not be reduced as earnings rose, so it would give to everybody *more* of an incentive to seek employment. It is the *present* system that discourages employment, because it pays unemployed people only *as long as* they do no paid work, and, even if there are fewer full-time job vacancies than there are people looking for them, the system still penalises people if they take part-time employment, start a small business, undertake training not specified by the Jobcentre, or commit themselves to voluntary work that would benefit both themselves and their communities: penalises them by withdrawing their benefits. A Citizen's Income would continue to be paid as earnings rose, so it would always be worth earning more; and it would continue to be paid if someone undertook a training course or voluntary work. It is thus a Citizen's Income and not the current system that is the way to improve incentives to work for an income. It is the way that we organise the benefits system now that discourages people from seeking employment.

# 12

## A Citizen's Income would increase women's incomes

Women now make up over 40% of the labour force, whereas in 1950 it was only 30%. Their earnings are often as important to the family as the man's, sometimes they are higher, and in many families the woman's earnings are the only earnings. In relation to Income Tax the woman and the man are both treated as independent human beings, but for means-tested benefits a joint claim has to be made. If the man becomes unemployed, the way in which the psychologies in many families work means that the woman is likely to give up her own employment – a process made more likely by the fact that the woman's earnings will reduce the means-tested benefits for which a joint claim has been made. So even if in theory the means-tested benefits system treats men and women as equals, in practice the woman's decisions are unlikely to be entirely her own.

A Citizen's Income would be an income for every *individual*, so whatever the circumstances of one partner, the other's Citizen's Income would not alter. Women are now more likely to want to earn an income, and the more equal treatment that a Citizen's Income would give to them would make it easier for them to do so.

If they had a Citizen's Income then there might be some women, and perhaps some men, who would decide to drop out of the employment market; and because tax allowances would be smaller or non-existent, there would not be quite the same incentive as there is now for one partner to earn small (untaxed) sums to supplement the other partner's earnings. However, the overall effect of a Citizen's Income would be to equalise the positions of women and men in the labour market by making it more possible for men to take part-time employment and more possible for women to keep their employment if their partners became unemployed. Although the psychological dynamics within the family might still mean that a man losing his job would precipitate the woman into giving up hers, the fact that her earnings would not affect the man's Citizen's Income would reduce the pressure for that to happen, and the greater sense of equality generated by individual Citizen's Incomes might do the rest.

Child Benefit goes to a child's main carer, and so usually to its mother. If a Citizen's Income were to be implemented then we would be in the interesting position of women with children having more control over the family's unconditional benefits than the man.

## 13

# A Citizen's Income would encourage new enterprise

The only problem with private incomes is that not everybody has one. Secure, continuous private incomes offer the security that enables people to try new activities. A Citizen's Income would provide for everybody the security that would make risk taking possible. An important result of a Citizen's Income pilot project in Namibia was the increase in economic activity among the lowest earners. The economic security that a small Citizen's Income had given to them enabled them to take the financial risks that new business ventures require.

Very few new businesses make a profit in the early months, and a Citizen's Income would reduce the amount of money that an individual or group of people would need to earn when a new business was in its early stages; and interestingly, a Citizen's Income would make possible the kind of small business that will never generate sufficient income to provide its participants with a living, such as the unprofitable village shops that are so essential to small communities.

New businesses are essential to a healthy, changing economy. For instance, new software companies have the flexibility to innovate in ways in which the well-established giants cannot. For the supply of new businesses to dry up would be a disaster, particularly in industries such as information and communication technology.

When your income is a low wage topped up by means-tested benefits, then it is difficult to think of doing something different, particularly when occasional additional earnings reduce the benefits. Someone who is unemployed has to put time into searching for a job or they risk losing their benefits, and occasional small earnings have to be reported so that benefits can be readjusted – with the frequent consequence that benefits payments are delayed. If a Citizen' Income were to replace means-tested benefits then none of this would be necessary. The small occasional earnings that a new business will often generate would not need to be reported to a benefits administrator; and no job-search requirements would distract attention from the demands of starting a business.

A small secure income would make it easier for people to take risks, and to stop doing what they were doing in order to do new things. The ways in which different individuals and families would find their lives changing would of course all be different, but for everyone the freedom to seek new employment patterns in order to do new things would be one of the many advantages of a Citizen's Income. For the sake of all the experiment waiting to happen, the idea should be given a try.

## 14

# A Citizen's Income would suit a technological economy

Nearly thirty years ago I visited a brickworks. I had expected dirt, activity, and sweat, but what I found was clinical, almost silent, and with just a few engineers around in case the machinery broke down.

Since the mechanisation of agriculture in the eighteenth century, new technology has separated production from labour and has thus reduced the labour market's ability to distribute the means of consumption. It is no surprise that we find engineers and scientists among those who have suggested that this new situation requires the State to distribute to its citizens the means of consumption. When a scientist or engineer sees a change in one part of a system, they ask what problems might arise in other parts of it, and then look for ways to optimise performance. [5]

Mechanisation and new information and communication technology are one of the reasons for money earned from production going increasingly to the owners of machines and technology, and decreasingly to employees. This would be simply a matter of social injustice if it were not also that poverty strangles our ability to buy goods and services and thus threatens the profits of industry and commerce. A Citizen's Income, funded by some of the money earned by machinery and technology, would distribute the means to consume goods and services to those who need to consume them; it would make more bearable the flexible labour market that a fast-changing technological society creates; and it would make it more beneficial for employees to learn the new skills that changing technology requires. Perhaps most importantly of all, at a time when preserving the earth's resources needs research and development as never before, maintaining demand for companies' goods and services will fund the research and development that will be needed if we are to prepare for a carbon-free economy.

The world is changing. The question is not 'How can we stop it?', but 'How can we make sure that the changes improve our life together and our lives as individuals?' A Citizen's Income would be one way to make that happen.

## 15

# A Citizens Income would work well with a National Minimum Wage or a Living Wage

A National Minimum Wage (NMW) ensures that bad employers do not experience a competitive advantage; and because it encourages organisations to make the most of expensive labour by ensuring that their workforces are well trained and that production processes are efficient, and because increasing wages can reduce staff turnover, an NMW can improve the efficiency of both industry and public services. At the levels at which NMWs are usually set in developed countries, they have little effect on employment levels. The same arguments apply to a Living Wage: that is, a wage level that generates an income sufficient to meet the Minimum Income Standards [6] required for full participation in the life of our society. However, a serious problem is that increases in an NMW are of little use to low-earning households. This is not the fault of the NMW; it is the fault of means-tested in-work benefits. As earnings rise, in-work benefits are reduced, so the household sees little improvement in its disposable income.

Here is not the place to argue over whether or not an NMW or a Living Wage is a good idea. What *is* important is that the debate over whether a Citizen's Income is a good idea, and the debate over whether an NMW or a Living Wage is a good idea are separate debates, and that a Citizen's Income and an NMW are not mutually exclusive alternatives, as has sometimes been alleged. Indeed, a Citizen's Income and an NMW would complement each other.

If everyone received a Citizen's Income then a proportion of their subsistence needs would be met before they entered the labour market. Their Citizen's Income would not function as a variable subsidy, as means-tested in-work benefits do by increasing as wages fall and thus accelerating a deterioration in wage levels; a Citizen's Income would function as a static subsidy, thus depressing wages less. An NMW can ensure that more of an employee's benefit to the company can end up with the employee, and a Living Wage would offer even more of such an effect.

At the same time, a Citizen's Income would provide a secure income foundation for any section of the workforce that found it more difficult to get employment in an employment market regulated by an NMW. And, because a Citizen's Income would not be withdrawn as earnings rose, a Citizen's Income would mean that a rise in the NMW or the Living Wage would benefit low earning households far more than it does now.

16

# A Citizen's Income would create a generally more efficient market in labour

An efficient market is one in which the price mechanism matches supply to demand; so an efficient employment market is one in which people get the employment that they want, in terms of number of hours, wage levels, skills required and so on, and employers get the employees that they want, in terms of number of hours, wage levels, skills required and so on.

The labour market is far from efficient. For most people, only full-time employment is an option, either because only a full-time job will provide sufficient income, or because if they are on means-tested benefits then they will be pressured into seeking full-time work, or because the high rate of benefits withdrawal makes it inefficient to seek part-time employment even if that is the kind of employment that would best suit someone's caring responsibilities. The current system is least efficient for second earners when a household's main earner loses their job and all that the second earner's earnings achieve is to reduce the household's benefits.

We can now sum up some of the reasons that we have already given and say that a Citizen's Income would generate the efficient employment that would benefit both employers and employees. As we have seen, today's benefits system interferes with people's employment decisions and it discourages skills acquisition – because making an income during full-time training is a problem, and because the higher wages promised by new skills can mean very little in the way of additional disposable income. A Citizen's Income would not be withdrawn as earnings rose, so part-time employment would become more worthwhile; someone's Citizen's Income would never be affected by their partner's employment status; and their Citizen's Income would provide an income during training, so encouraging skills acquisition, and would particularly encourage a combination of part-time employment and skills training.

Quite simply, a Citizen's Income would deliver a more efficient employment market. Employment supply would slowly adjust. Wages would move upwards for less desirable jobs, and maybe downwards for more desirable jobs. Hours offered would adjust – perhaps towards fewer full-time jobs and more part-time ones. A general rise in skills levels would bring employment into the country, and the quality of jobs would rise. Those who would prefer self-employment would be able to create it; those who wanted to start small businesses or cooperatives would be more able to do so; and those who wanted secure full-time employment would be able to achieve that. An efficient employment market could be good for everybody.

## 17

# A Citizen's Income would encourage training and education

A healthy economy and a healthy society need people to be educated and trained, so that we can earn a living for ourselves and our families, and so that manufacturing, service provision, and the processing of information can be undertaken by highly skilled individuals.

To satisfy these needs we run a patchwork of university and college education, apprenticeships, company training schemes, self-financed and company-financed courses, and governments contracting out to private companies the training schemes that people without employment are required to attend – and who risk losing their benefits if they do not do so. Most of this diversity will continue, and it should; but if it is to continue then we shall need to sort out the patchwork of financial provision for people undertaking training or education. Course fees and the loss of income during courses are serious disincentives, so people fail to reach their potential as creative human beings, and society and the economy are deprived of the new skills that they could have developed, or people pay for education with loans and end up with unrepayable debt.

How should education and training be paid for: by grants, or loans, or industrial sponsorship of individuals and/ or institutions? A Citizen's Income would not completely solve the funding dilemma, but it would at least provide a secure financial foundation for students; and because someone's Citizen's Income would continue whatever their relationship with the employment market, and would not stop during periods of education (as the tax allowance does if someone ceases to earn an income), it would encourage people to undertake part-time or full-time education or training both after leaving school and throughout their lives, and would make it much easier for everyone to make rational choices about the best kind of education and training for them. For many 18-year-olds, part-time education and part-time employment might be a better option than either full-time employment or full-time education, but this is a combination that is currently quite difficult to manage financially. It would be far easier to manage if a Citizen's Income and part-time employment were between them providing sufficient income to avoid the young adult amassing serious levels of debt.

By giving to young students and trainees a secure income on which they could build with grants, loans, and sponsorship, and by helping people to participate in education and training later in life, a Citizen's Income would give to us the skilled workforce that we shall need for a healthy economy, and the well-educated community that we shall need for a healthy society.

## 18

# A Citizen's Income would maintain demand

It is of course an interesting question as to whether we *should* attempt to maintain demand. If demand for manufactured goods rises, then pollution increases, we use up scarce non-renewable resources, carbon emissions rise, and climate change worsens. If demand for meat products rises then the same occurs. But demand for renewable energy causes carbon emissions to fall; and demand for organic vegetables displaces other demand, so again carbon emissions would fall. Demand for literature and music downloads contributes both to individual and to social cultural development, and has little impact on the level of carbon emissions.

The poverty trap and the unemployment trap constrain demand. If disposable income is not going to rise when wages rise, then employees will not seek to increase their wages and their disposable incomes will not rise; but if a rise in wages, or the finding of employment, *will* increase someone's disposable income, then they are more likely to seek higher wages or to look for employment, their disposable income is more likely to rise, and they will inject new demand into the economy. This would be particularly true of a Citizen's Income funded by government money creation rather than by adjustments to tax allowances and means-tested and other benefits; but either way, a Citizen's Income would contribute to an increase in demand.

People with low disposable incomes are more likely to spend money into the local economy than to save it, whereas higher earners are more likely to save money, and their purchases are less likely to benefit local businesses. Because those who suffer most from the poverty and unemployment traps are among the lowest earners, and because they would experience most of the benefit of a transition to a Citizen's Income – because it would be their marginal deduction rates that would fall, and it would be they who would see more rapid increases in disposable income as their earnings rose – a Citizen's Income would generate additional demand in local economies. [7]

A Citizen's Income would also maintain and satisfy a rather different kind of demand. By making it more possible for people to be employed part time, or to take on more flexible employment patterns, a Citizen's Income would make it easier for people to care for elderly or disabled relatives and to undertake voluntary work in their communities. Meeting this demand is at least as important as meeting any other kind.

# 19

## A Citizen's Income would create opportunities

Without opportunity there can be no social or individual wellbeing. Opportunity to be educated, to work (both paid and unpaid), to create a home, to develop relationships: these are all necessary to a flourishing community in which everyone can participate, and where these opportunities do not exist, then poverty is the result.

We have seen enormous strides in the distribution of opportunity during the past century: in education, training, health and safety at work, racial and sexual equality, public health, healthcare, and housing quality. However, we dare not stand still, for in a fast-changing world we must constantly create new opportunities, for only by doing that will we be able to abolish poverty of all kinds, and keep it abolished.

The UK's healthcare and education systems, free at the point of use (even if increasingly provided by the private sector), are essential universal underpinnings of opportunity, and where these do not exist opportunities are severely restricted. Similarly, the universal franchise and equality before the law are essential foundations for everyone's opportunity to take part in the creation of justice.

But why exempt income from this general conviction that equal opportunity is good for society? Why provide healthcare, education, and the vote on a universal and non-withdrawable basis, and not the most basic requirement of a community: money to live on? [8] A high equal income, as a right, might prove something of a disincentive to seek employment, and might make it difficult to get essential work done, but Sir Ralf Dahrendorf made the point that an equal *foundational* income is as necessary to a civil society as is equality before the law. [9] A relatively small Citizen's Income would not damage incentives to seek or create paid employment – indeed, it would increase them. A Citizen's Income should therefore be provided on the same basis as free healthcare and education and argued for in the same way: that equality of opportunity is the way to justice and wealth, both individual and corporate.

If we regard the provision of opportunity through education and healthcare for all to be essential to a civilised society, then should we not also regard it as essential to provide that most basic of all foundations of opportunity: an income to live on?

## 20

# A Citizen's Income would encourage further economic evolution

Money evolves all the time. An important recent evolution is credit cards, which enable us to create money so that we can organise consumption efficiently. But new financial mechanisms can create new problems. Uncontrolled credit card debt can cause human misery, and the computer-selling of shares can cause stock-market crashes. Banks lend by increasing balances in customers' accounts, and by doing that they create new money; and when the loan is repaid the money disappears again. It was largely the uncontrolled way in which banks made loans that were unlikely to be repaid, and the ways in which those loans were treated as assets and then sold, that caused the recent financial crisis.

More positively, if money is a human creation, with no absolute laws but only temporary conventions, then there is no reason why we should not ask what kind of society and economy we want, and then make money behave accordingly.

There is an argument for only governments to be able to create money and to spend it into the economy – perhaps as a Citizen's Income. Another intriguing idea is that we should encourage more local authorities to create their own distinctive and convertible currencies (as baby-sitting circles create tokens that can be exchanged for cash) and to pay them into their local economies as local Citizen's Incomes.

The benefits system looks so complicated that governments hesitate to attempt genuine reform. Because a Citizen's Income could be established easily, without generating new problems, it might encourage governments to change other systems previously thought untouchable, such as the way in which money is created by the banks, or the indicators that we use to measure 'growth': Gross National Product and Gross Domestic Product. These are highly arbitrary and do not tell us much about our real wealth, so change is overdue. Establishing a Citizen's Income might also inspire new taxes, such as an international financial transaction tax to put a brake on currency speculation – and to pay for a Citizen's Income.

Recent governments have questioned many orthodoxies, but money creation, and taxation and benefits, have never experienced the kinds of serious questioning and major overhauls that they require. A Citizen's Income would be a minor administrative adjustment that would constitute a major benefits reform, and it would prompt similar new thinking about the behaviour of money, about taxation, about economic indicators, and about much else. It would be an important new step in its own right, but it might be just as important for the other new thinking that it would encourage.

## 21

# A Citizen's Income would form a new link between income and production

Because the return on capital is greater than the growth of the economy,[10] the gap between wages and the proceeds of productivity is increasing. Less of the proceeds from production is now recycled back into industry via wages and consumption. The results are more people on low pay and means-tested benefits, fewer people feeling connected to the economy, and manufacturing and service industries suffering contractions in demand.

A Citizen's Income would address this problem. It would connect everyone to the economy in the same way; it would reduce the effects of the unemployment and poverty traps and so would enable every individual and every family to participate in the economic and social life of the community through the kinds of employment and self-employment that they wished to undertake; and it could create a new link between income and industry by paying a universal income out of the proceeds of industry (perhaps via a tax on profits or dividends). A Citizen's Income would thus recreate for everyone a close connection between the growth of the economy and individual consumption.

The economy's task is not to provide everyone with a job. Its task is to provide everyone with an income, and with the opportunity for creating a larger income if that is needed. With a Citizen's Income we would discover exactly what mix of employment and unpaid activity people do want, and we might find that lots of people do not want a full-time paid job, but that they do want a part-time job and the opportunity to do other things with their lives, some of which might be paid and some of which might not.

There is no reason why human labour should do many of the repetitive tasks that can be done by machines, nor why the only normative route for money should be through earned incomes to consumption spending and so back to industry and into further earnings. We need a variety of normative routes to match the flexibility that we already experience in the labour market: a variety of routes that will support both a diverse money economy and a diverse gift or voluntary economy.

Only if we break the link between income and paid work shall we find new ways to create and distribute income and wealth; and a Citizen's Income will therefore be seen to have been an essential means of creating the new links between income, industry, and consumption that we now require.

# 22

# A Citizen's Income would break a logjam

As the world's economy has developed, 'logjams' have occurred. Technology has lain idle, creativity has gone to waste, poverty has increased in the midst of abundance, and no amount of tinkering can remedy the situation – until a new 'key concept' has emerged that has enabled new ideas and new technology to create new kinds of wealth. Coinage, paper money, double-entry book-keeping, the limited liability company: these and other key concepts have freed the economy from stagnation and have stimulated new creative development, which has then itself stagnated until the next new key concept arrives.

The evolutions of life and of science offer parallels. Increasing complexity has produced stagnation, turbulence has set in, and then some new development has set the process moving again. New developments that have set life's evolution, scientific progress, or the economy free, have usually been prefigured by developments bearing some but not all of their characteristics; they have been symptoms of change as well as its cause; they have created revolutions with immense social implications; and in science and the economy they have had passionate advocates and equally passionate detractors – and, once in place, people have wondered why it all took so long.[11]

We have again reached a crisis (both a disaster and an opportunity): technology lying idle, human creativity frustrated, wealth flowing from poor to rich, and finite resources uncontrollably exploited. Minor changes, such as new regulations for the banks, will alleviate the stresses for a time, and we shall muddle along; but we are still waiting for the next new key concept.

A Citizen's Income might be just what is required. It has emerged at a time of economic stagnation and social and political change; there are forerunners (Child Benefit and the National Health Service); it is a symptom of change; it has its passionate advocates and its equally passionate detractors; it would create an economic and a social revolution; and, once in place, we would all wonder why it took so long.

What matters, of course, is whether the new key concept will be good for us. Whether all previous evolutions have been is debatable. (Was it really such a good idea to enable building societies to demutualise?) But a Citizen's Income clearly is a good idea, so it is a key concept that we should embrace.

## 23

# A Citizen's Income would encourage a gift economy

Wealth is not just money – and in fact money is not wealth at all, for it is simply a means of exchange. Wealth is health, education, a stimulating and clean environment, an adequate home to live in, care when we need it, good relationships within the family and between neighbours, creativity and participation in the workplace, opportunities for leisure, and a host of other things; and the creation of all of this wealth is a complex process involving both a money economy and an informal 'gift' economy in which people give their time and labour without financial incentive or reward.

A Citizen's Income would shift the balance between the money and gift economies in different directions for different people. Some people would take the reduced poverty and unemployment traps as an invitation to be more active in the money economy, while others would use their Citizen's Income to enable them to reduce the hours that they spend in the money economy and to give more time to their family, to community activity, and perhaps to leisure and educational activity for themselves. By having more choice, both groups would be more 'wealthy'.

A group for whom a Citizen's Income would be particularly useful would be those currently without employment and on means-tested benefits. If your benefits income requires permanent 'availability for work', attendance at the Jobcentre, and compulsory training courses and unpaid work, then commitment to voluntary activity can be difficult; and, perhaps more importantly, if your means-tested benefits come loaded with stigma, then it takes a strong personality to engage deeply with voluntary work. Because everybody would receive a Citizen's Income, it would carry no stigma, so a great deal of energy would be released for voluntary and caring activity.

Thus wealth of all kinds would increase, and, because more people would be able to give time and energy to such activity, we would see *new* kinds of wealth creation – in both the gift and the money economies – and more kinds of wealth on the boundary between the two economies: voluntary activity leading to new activity in the money economy, and new activity in the money economy leading to new voluntary activity.

Thus a Citizen's Income would encourage caring for family members and neighbours, self-education networks, sports and leisure activities, self-build houses, and a host of other kinds of wealth creation, and a Citizen's Income would thus remake what we mean by the word 'wealth' so that its normal meaning became the one that I have suggested for it.

# B
# A CHANGING
# SOCIETY

24

# A Citizen's Income would have an individual assessment unit

Each individual would receive their own Citizen's Income. This would be good for families and for personal autonomy; but it would also make the administration of a Citizen's Income extremely easy to manage. Means-tested benefits normally pay less to couples than they pay in total to two people living alone, so administrators need to keep track of who is living with whom. A Citizen's Income would require none of this administrative effort, and it would save civil servants delving into people's intimate relationships, something that they usually have no wish to do.

It is important to emphasise the fact that the individual assessment unit is essential to a Citizen's Income, because in some descriptions of schemes called 'Basic Income' or 'Citizen's Income' this principle has been lost. Steven Webb's 1990 'Basic Income' scheme [1] is based on the household (hence the inverted commas), and he claims that this would save money. First, it would save very little (and in particular it would save nothing for claimants still on means-tested benefits, for their lower joint 'Basic Income' would entitle them to higher means-tested benefits than would two genuine individual Citizen's Incomes); and secondly, the scheme would require civil servants to collect information on the personal relationships of everyone receiving the household-based 'Basic Income'. At the moment, the UK Government collects information on the personal relationships of means-tested benefits claimants. The UK used to have a higher tax allowance for married couples, which meant that married couples paid less tax than they would have paid as two single individuals (an interesting inversion of the lower benefits paid to couples). This higher tax allowance was abolished in April 2000, and now only if couples receive income jointly (such as rent on property owned jointly) does their relationship have any relevance to their tax affairs. If a 'Basic Income' were to be paid to households, then the Government would need information on the personal relationships of *every citizen*. This would be as politically unacceptable as it would be administratively difficult, and the scheme would become both unpopular and unworkable.

A Citizen's Income is an unconditional, automatic and non-withdrawable income for every individual citizen. Not only would such a Citizen's Income enable everyone to create their own relationships without intrusive coercion from benefits regulations and officials, but it would offer administrative efficiency the like of which we have never seen before.

# 25

# A Citizen's Income would suit more fluid family structures

From 1976 to 1978 I worked on the public counter in Brixton's Supplementary Benefit Office and experienced at first hand the workings of means-tested benefits: a system that was in need of reform then, and is even more so today.

A serious problem was that there were never enough of the long treasury tags to link together the casepapers of individuals who were involved with each other. Papers had to be linked together because people cohabiting were a household and so could only submit one claim for benefits; because if two people lived together as husband and wife then they received between them less in means-tested benefits than they would have done as two individuals; and because the calculation of the household's benefit entitlement had to take into account the income of every household member. This is all still true of in-work and out-of-work means-tested benefits, except that today it is staff using computers who are trying to link people's claims together, rather than staff walking around offices looking for casepapers and the tags with which to connect them.

The system is not designed for changing family structures (a man leaving, another coming, and then another – and with which of the two is she cohabiting, and who is the lodger?). This is all bound to be inefficient when families change rapidly, and when there is no such thing as a normal family. The complexity has always made computerisation of means-tested benefits difficult, and is one of the reasons for the transition to the UK's new means-tested Universal Credit being so difficult to manage.

A Citizen's Income could be a step in the right direction, even if not a total solution to the problem, because it would be paid to every individual at the same rate, and because it would take no account whatsoever of family structure. The cohabitation rule would still apply to people who continued to need residual means-tested benefits, but for many of those families the ability to escape from the unemployment trap and the cohabitation rule, and the freedom from intrusion that a Citizen's Income would offer, might between them persuade them to add to their Citizen's Incomes with earnings rather than with means-tested benefits.

The only way for tax and benefits systems to cope with fluid family patterns is for tax and benefits to be calculated separately for every individual, whether living alone or not. In the UK, Income Tax moved in this direction twenty years ago. It is time for the benefits system to do the same.

## 26

# A Citizen's Income would provide freedom around relationships

Separation and divorce are now more common than they once were, and the change is largely because many women are now more independent financially and are not held in unhappy relationships by the prospect of poverty should they leave them. Whatever our views on divorce, this new independence makes everything more honest. Financial arrangements are only one part of a couple's relationship, and they should never be the most important factor in the survival or the quality of that relationship. But there are still many women without any financial independence from their partners, often because they are caring for children and are not employed outside the home. A Citizen's Income would give to such women a new independence that would help them to make decisions about a relationship's future according to factors other than money.

At the moment, two people on means-tested benefits might decide not to form a household because their total income would drop if they did so; or a woman on means-tested benefits might decide not to move in with a man in full-time employment because if she did then she would lose her benefits and thus lose the small financial independence that the current benefits system has given to her. Should people's living arrangements be determined to this extent by social security regulations? Would it not be better if such regulations did not affect people's relationships? Then relationships would be chosen for reasons of physical attraction, mutual compatibility, the care of children, the care of relatives, mutual support, or whatever other reasons seemed right to the people involved.

Particularly bad for relationships is the bureaucratic intrusion that goes with means-tested benefits. Because personal relationships affect claims for means-tested benefits, benefits office staff need to know about the relationships in which means-tested benefits claimants find themselves – which means enquiring about the intimate details of relationships and seeking evidence about those details. In the UK, Her Majesty's Revenue and Customs staff do not interfere in taxpayers' relationships in the same way as they do in relationships in families receiving means-tested Working Tax Credits. They should not be interfering at all.

As long as we have means-tested benefits they will skew people's relationships and interfere in them. A Citizen's Income would neither skew nor interfere in relationships, but instead would increase people's choices, and would encourage decision making based on things more relevant to the relationships concerned. In this way a Citizen's Income would increase the formation rates, the survival rates, and the quality of people's relationships.

# 27

## A Citizen's Income would increase our autonomy

We now expect to choose our way of life: our employment, our pastimes, where we live, to whom we relate, and how we behave socially, sexually, and financially. This has its problems (mainly in terms of broken relationships), but personal autonomy is in general a good thing because it creates a diverse society in which people can make their own decisions, carry out their own projects, and learn to get along together in a fast-changing world.

The problem with our current benefits system is that it does not give to us the necessary autonomy, but rather traps us into prescribed family and financial patterns. A Citizen's Income would give to us greater autonomy financially, and it would also be a catalyst, creating further autonomy. Rather than promoting any particular family or labour-market pattern, it would be neutral towards all of them, and would actively promote the ability of an individual to choose how much paid work to do and how much unpaid, and to choose to whom to relate and for how long.

There will be those who do not think such autonomy to be desirable because it is not biased in favour of their own particular vision of the good society, the good family, or the good lifestyle; but they should rethink. A Citizen's Income would enable people to choose their own social, family or lifestyle structures without reference to benefits regulations. This would mean that moral convictions would become more important, not less. To take one example: a Citizen's Income would give greater autonomy to non-earning partners in a couple because for the first time they would have an income of their own (unlike Child Benefit, which is their income because they receive it for their children). Such financial autonomy would not make an enormous difference to the distribution of wealth or power within most relationships, but in some it would give to the non-earning partner a sense of autonomy and might provoke a rethink on the part of both partners as to what their relationship is about and how it should evolve into the future.

A Citizen's Income would reflect the greater personal autonomy that we already have, and it would promote greater autonomy. One definition of good social policy is that it should reflect and promote change in society, and on such a definition a Citizen's Income would seem to be very good social policy.

## 28

# A Citizen's Income would make diverse life plans a possibility

For thirty-four years I worked full time in the Church of England's ministry in wonderfully interesting parishes in South London. Five times I was granted periods of study leave of varying lengths so that I could write articles and books on metaphysics, the Citizen's Income debate, the history of workplace chaplaincy, and the management of religious and faith-based organisations. I have now retired early and so am able to spend more time on research at the London School of Economics and on being Director of the Citizen's Income Trust – a voluntary task that for twenty years I have been able to fit in around work in the parish. All of this has been a huge privilege. I am conscious that too few people have the opportunity for such diverse and fulfilling work, and that far too few have the opportunity to take sabbaticals – periods of time for education, creativity, and new tasks – either because their employment does not allow for it, or because giving up employment in order to take a sabbatical would result in a substantial loss of income.

If we were to receive a Citizen's Income instead of personal tax allowances and means-tested benefits, then the change in disposable income on losing part or all of an earned income would not be so great, and taking periods out of paid employment would become more of a possibility. We would be better educated and better trained, and more able to plan for the changes in careers and occupations that a changing economy will require. A Citizen's Income would not achieve all of this on its own, and grants and sponsorship would continue to be important ways of financing further education and training, but a Citizen's Income would contribute to the process both financially and psychologically: financially, by providing a continuing income, and psychologically, because a Citizen's Income would be a statement by society that financial support is a gift as well as something that we earn. The change in mind-set would be as important as the continuing income in enabling many of us to think about seeking new experiences and new intellectual activity.

To be able to plan when to be employed full time and when part time, when to choose a period for further education, and when to take time out of employment to look after children or elderly relatives would enable all of us to create our own life plans, and would result in more fulfilled individuals, and in a society and an economy more able to adapt as the world changes around us.

## 29

# A Citizen's Income would deliver greater equality and independence for women

If a man becomes unemployed and finds himself on means-tested benefits, then most of his partner's income will be deducted from his benefits. There will often be little financial benefit from her staying in employment, and in some families she will experience psychological pressure to leave her job. For a woman who becomes unemployed, the situation can be different but equally damaging, for she loses her income and also the benefit of her personal tax allowance, and often becomes totally dependent on her earning partner because she cannot claim means-tested benefits in her own right.

Our benefits system still assumes that two members of a couple wish to be financially dependent on each other. My wife would be justifiably furious if her income (which is higher than mine) were to be paid to me rather than to her, and I would not be too pleased if it was the other way round; yet means-tested benefits still assume that the whole of a family's benefits income will be paid to one household member.

A Citizen's Income would help to right such injustices, because each adult household member would receive their own Citizen's Income; and if the man lost his job, and if the family's Citizen's Incomes and his partner's earnings added up to enough for them all to live on, then no claim for means-tested benefits would be required. A Citizen's Income would also prevent a woman from becoming totally dependent on her partner if she became unemployed. In all of these cases, the damage to the family would be less than it is now, and we might see fewer relationship breakdowns caused by unemployment.

Not only would a Citizen's Income contribute to both equality and independence for women, but it would do this by means that do not need to be policed, unlike many other attempts to create greater equality between women and men. A Citizen's Income would also be a statement of the equality of every citizen, whatever the source of their income. Again, greater equality will have been created without the need for enforcement.

In addition to greater autonomy in the economy and in the labour market, a Citizen's Income would offer to women greater autonomy, and greater ability to carry out diverse life plans. Just for once, we would not be looking at a zero sum game. Greater autonomy for women, and greater autonomy for everybody, would go hand in hand, creating one more equality between women and men.

## 30

# A Citizen's Income would provide greater equality for people living with disabilities

Would a Citizen's Income change things much for people living with disabilities, or would it simply add to the mosaic of provision already in place? Someone living with disability or chronic illness needs money and services – different amounts of money, and different services, for every individual. These are usually provided by a mixture of government benefits and services and cash payments. A Citizen's Income would not change any of this. For someone unable to seek employment, their Citizen's Income would simply replace a proportion of their current benefits.

The situation would be different for people able to undertake small numbers of hours of appropriate employment. At the moment, administering the current mixture of benefits and services alongside fluctuating low wages is far from easy. It is often easier not to be employed, or to work in the informal economy and not declare earnings. If someone's Citizen's Income, along with local authority cash and services and small earnings, were sufficient to live on, then they might decide to do without government benefits and the accompanying disability assessments. Then the only declaration of earnings required would be a tax return. No longer would earnings need to be declared to benefits administrators. Life would be more legal and a lot simpler, and the same mechanism that would float numerous families off means-tested benefits would be operating among people with disabilities too.

A Citizen's Income would not only provide people with disabilities with more choices in relation to employment, and with a secure income floor: it would also integrate them with the rest of society in new ways. Everyone would receive a Citizen's Income, which would help to integrate people with disabilities and chronic illnesses with the rest of society; the enhanced employment options that a Citizen's Income would deliver would also contribute to social integration; and the way in which a Citizen's Income can float people off means-tested benefits would apply to people with disabilities in the same way as it applies to everyone else.

The trend is towards supplying cash rather than services so that people with disabilities can pay for their own care and generally exercise more autonomy. A Citizen's Income would also supply cash – unconditionally and non-withdrawably – and so would enhance the trend towards financial independence.

Above all, a Citizen's Income would increase people's ability to choose the mixture of paid and unpaid activity that suited them, which would contribute positively both to disposable incomes and to social inclusion. The same would be true for many other people, too.

# 31

# A Citizen's Income would make carers' lives easier

A 'carer' here is anybody informally caring for someone, of whatever age, with substantial caring needs. Most carers are worse off than they would be if they did not have caring responsibilities, because they cannot earn much and because caring costs money (for necessary equipment, or because only local shopping is possible). In the UK, Carer's Allowance offers some compensation, but much of the amount received is deducted from means-tested benefits (including Working Tax Credits and Universal Credit), so many families receive little overall benefit. A Citizen's Income would lift many carers who get Carer's Allowance off means-tested benefits, enabling them to live on their Citizen's Income, their Carer's Allowance, and whatever occasional earnings their caring responsibilities might permit. Whatever provision a country's benefits system makes for carers, a Citizen's Income could only help.

Many carers who have cared for others for a long period will have no occupational or private pension. In the UK, because since 1978 carers have had their National Insurance Contributions paid for them, many will receive a Basic State Pension, and in the future the Single Tier State Pension: a non-withdrawable pension for each individual as a right of citizenship. (The Single Tier State Pension is not entirely unconditional, because only someone with 35 years of contributions or contribution credits will receive the full pension.) Some other countries already have true Citizen's Pensions. [2]

An important psychological advantage of a Citizen's Income would be that both carer and cared for would receive the same Citizen's Income – and the same Citizen's Income as every other adult in the country. No longer would carers' financial situations be entirely different from those without caring responsibilities, and no longer would cared for and carer experience entirely different financial situations. Carers' social inclusion would be enhanced.

Should carers receive an increased Citizen's Income? No – because this would destroy the Citizen's Income's simplicity. It would be better to retain such special provisions as the UK's Carer's Allowance so that bureaucratic involvement in people's lives remains entirely separate from Citizen's Income administration. Some carers might then be able to live on their Citizen's Income and on part-time or occasional earnings, and might therefore be able to avoid the administrative complexities of both the Carer's Allowance and means-tested benefits. For their sakes, and for everybody else's, the administration of Citizen's Incomes needs to be radically simple. Conditional supplements will need to be administered separately.

## 32

# A Citizen's Income would benefit people without homes

Why *are* there so many people without homes, in inadequate accommodation, or in bed and breakfast paid for by local authorities? In the UK, too few homes are being built, social housing that is sold off is less efficiently occupied, central government has prevented local authorities from building new housing, and relationship breakdown multiplies the number of homes required.

And when somebody *is* homeless, what are they to live on? In theory, the current benefits system leaves nobody out as long as they obey the rules and fulfil job-search and other conditions: but the system is not designed for somebody without a fixed address.

A Citizen's Income would of course be paid to people of no fixed abode in the same way as it would be paid to everybody else, and because its administration could be automated, and it could be drawn anywhere in the country, it would not pose the same administrative problems as current means-tested benefits. Single homeless people would be able to live on their Citizen's Income, and for homeless families their Citizen's Incomes would be a secure income not dependent on a fixed address, which would reduce the problems experienced when homeless families move rapidly from place to place.

But a Citizen's Income would also make it less likely that people would become homeless in the first place. A Citizen's Income would give to family members greater economic independence and would therefore improve their relationships with each other. A Citizen's Income would make it financially beneficial for people to live together (unlike now, when people on means-tested benefits who cohabit have their benefit reduced). A Citizen's Income would enable families to climb out of the poverty that is often the precursor to homelessness. And a Citizen's Income would provide a secure financial base, whatever else was happening to a family's benefits, enabling the rent to be paid when other benefits are stopped, reduced, or delayed. Unfortunately, a Citizen's Income would not directly result in more homes being built.

But should we simply give money, unconditionally, to homeless people? The results of a 2009 pilot project in London suggest that we should. Simply to give money, unconditionally, is a highly effective way of enabling homeless people to get roofs over their heads and to turn their lives around. [3] A Citizen's Income would not solve the homelessness crisis, but it would make homelessness less common, and it would provide a secure income for people who are homeless. For these reasons alone it is worth trying.

## 33

# A Citizen's Income would provide a secure income in old age

In the UK, we shall soon see many pensioners escaping from means-testing. Until now, everyone who has paid National Insurance Contributions has received a Basic State Pension, and this, along with a State Second Pension, an occupational pension, or another private pension income, has generally provided sufficient to live on in old age. For those without private or occupational pension provision – because of long-term caring responsibilities, or because their employment has not provided pension schemes, or because low self-employed earnings have not been enough to enable them to pay pension contributions – means-tested benefits have been available. The problem is that savings and other income reduce the amount of means-tested benefits, so there has been little incentive to save towards the costs of old age.

The new Single Tier State Pension will increase the level of the Basic State Pension to the level of means-tested benefits, so that, after a transition period, people's small savings or small private or occupational pensions will no longer reduce their state pension. (Because housing costs vary so much across the country, means-tested Housing Benefit will still be required.) The Single Tier State Pension is not quite a Citizen's Pension [4] because to receive the full amount a pensioner will need a thirty-five year record of contributions or credits, but it is a significant step in the right direction.

In many European countries it might be better to retain the current structure of social insurance pensions and to establish a relatively small Citizen's Pension alongside them; but whatever the context, a Citizen's Income in old age would reduce anxiety among those approaching retirement, would be electorally popular, would be affordable, would enable many now on means-tested benefits to earn small incomes and thus get themselves off means-tested benefits, and would be a statement that elderly people are members of society, something that not all elderly people now feel.

If retirement is a well-earned rest from active participation in society, then income in retirement should be by way of pensions that we pay for; but if retirement is an invitation to new activities and new ways of belonging to society, then society should provide an unconditional income in old age. Because retirement is both a disengagement and a re-engagement, a mixture of state and private provision is appropriate. The Single Tier State Pension will enable this to happen, and an entirely unconditional Citizen's Pension would be even better at it.

## 34

# A Citizen's Income would provide a pre-retirement income

Retired people receive pensions: but what about those approaching retirement age?

Increasing longevity and the increasing cost of pension provision mean that in many countries the state pension age is rising, and will no doubt continue to rise; and, at the same time, experience of retirement is becoming more diverse. If people retire early then there might be a reduced occupational or other private pension, but there will be no state pension. Many will find a part-time job with which to fill the income gap, and this can be a useful stepping stone into retirement; but some will find themselves on means-tested benefits – a system now characterised in the UK by a bit of flexibility in relation to the pre-retired, but it still assumes that men and women will continue in full-time employment until the state pension age.

A Citizen's Income would make everything more flexible, because it would be paid during full-time employment and part-time employment, during semi-retirement, and during retirement (as a Citizen's Pension). Other pension income would still be needed, but the whole of one's income from the State would no longer be determined by which side of a somewhat arbitrary retirement age you happened to be.

For many people, the ideal retirement process is to move from full-time to part-time employment and then maybe to stop altogether. A Citizen's Income would reflect and encourage this trend towards more flexible retirement because it would make the state pension age even less significant than it is now. All that would happen at the designated age would be that someone's Citizen's Income would rise to the level of the Citizen's Pension: and because everyone would have a Citizen's Income, we would see a variety of retirement patterns, the most common being a gradual retirement from paid employment.

The flexible 'decade of retirement', and flexible retirement, are becoming the norm, but few concrete proposals have been made to encourage the process and to enable it to serve the needs of citizens. A Citizen's Income would fill part of the income gap, and would go further by offering people the opportunity to vary their participation in the labour market at any age. It would put an end to anomalies and, if the pre-retirement Citizen's Income were large enough, it would minimise means-testing, tackle poverty, encourage saving for old age, help to make flexible retirement less of a dream and more of a reality, and prevent the poverty in old age that stems partly at least from the complexity and stigma of the present web of means-tested benefits.

# 35

# A Citizen's Income would promote social inclusion

There is plenty of social exclusion. People on low incomes have less choice than others: about where to live, about housing tenure, about what to eat, about children's schooling, about leisure activities, and about much more besides. People on low incomes find it difficult to participate in the social activities in which many other people can participate. Children's extracurricular activities cost money; going to the cinema or the theatre costs money; going on holiday or out for the day costs money; sharing a drink or a restaurant meal with friends or colleagues costs money... When there is inadequate money, difficult choices have to be made.

Social exclusion can be particularly disadvantageous for children. Music lessons, uniformed organisations, school trips, summer holidays, days out, computers, and the games, toys, clothes and shoes currently in fashion, all cost money. For children, exclusion from the activities in which other children are participating can result in stigma and lower social capital, and can therefore lead to further social exclusion later in life.

Means-tested benefits exacerbate social exclusion. For someone to receive means-tested benefits is a statement that they need help, that they have not succeeded, that they do not belong in the mainstream of society. At the same time, means-tested benefits prevent families from earning their way out of poverty, and so perpetuate social exclusion which to some extent means-tested benefits have helped to create. In the UK it was always hoped that Working Tax Credits would not be experienced in this way, but their slow replacement by Universal Credit means that employees on means-tested benefits and unemployed people on means-tested benefits will soon all be in the same boat: [5] all socially excluded and stigmatised by virtue of receiving the same exclusionary means-tested benefits.

Social exclusion has many faces and many causes, and no single prescription will enable everyone suffering from some form of social exclusion to experience social inclusion instead: but a Citizen's Income would offer to many individuals and families a deeper inclusion than they currently experience. They would be receiving the same benefit as everyone else, they would be more able to seek and to find suitable employment, and they would be more able to turn additional earnings into additional disposable income. All of these effects of a Citizen's Income would improve social inclusion, and together they could generate a substantial inclusionary effect for millions of people.

## 36

# A Citizen's Income would enhance social mobility

Inequality matters less if people in one position in society can move easily to another: if by gaining skills they can access better quality employment, or if by working hard they can improve their family's financial situation. Inequality matters much more if social mobility is not a possibility, because then disadvantaged people are trapped in their disadvantage.

Societies are becoming less mobile. In many developed countries the employment market is bifurcating into good jobs (well-paid and with good conditions) and lousy jobs (badly paid and with poor conditions). If people in lousy jobs are on in-work means-tested benefits that are withdrawn rapidly as earnings rise, then they are unable to increase their disposable incomes by earning more, and so remain trapped on their low incomes: whereas people in good jobs who are not on in-work means-tested benefits will experience much lower withdrawal rates and will be able fairly easily to improve their disposable incomes by earning more. This mechanism must be one of the major reasons for the way in which a bifurcating employment market is delivering a bifurcating society.

A further mechanism is a similar bifurcation in skills accumulation. Lousy jobs rarely come with high quality training attached, so employees find it difficult to progress to a better job within the same company or in a different one. Good jobs often come with high quality training attached, giving access to promotion prospects within the company, or to a variety of opportunities with other employers. Public sector and voluntary sector employers are better at providing training in their lower paid employments, and they are more likely to be paying a Living Wage, so mobility can be more of a possibility: but now that so many services are outsourced to multinational companies, this route to social mobility is less available than it used to be. Yes, high quality education is available outside the workplace: but it costs money and it costs time, and money and time are in shorter supply among people in lousy jobs than they are among people in good jobs. A recent OECD report [6] states that low incomes are restricting human capital accumulation, and therefore educational opportunities, skills development, and social mobility. It calls for well-designed methods for redistributing income.

We used to speak of a ladder that people could climb from one social position to another. The problem today is that there are some rungs missing. A Citizen's Income would put them back in.

## 37

# A Citizen's Income would reduce stigma

Stigma is the sense of shame that people suffer if they find themselves in situations of which society does not approve.

When I worked in Brixton's Supplementary Benefit office I had to persuade elderly people to claim the Supplementary Pension to which they were entitled. They felt that the UK's Basic State Pension was something that they or their husbands had paid for (even if it is not strictly an insurance scheme), and that the means-tested supplement was a hand-out that they could only receive with a sense of shame. The UK's Minister for Pensions is changing that. The new Single Tier State Pension will mean that most pensioners will no longer need a means-tested supplement (although Housing Benefit and Council Tax Support will sometimes still be required).

An important source of the stigma that unemployed people experience is other people's fears that they might one day be in the same position: fears that generate the language of 'scroungers' and 'skivers'. The stigma experienced by receiving means-tested benefits that other people do not receive is exacerbated by earnings rules (which require declaration of a spouse's earnings) and cohabitation rules (which require people to reveal personal details). A sense of vulnerability to officials and their questions also heightens stigma, as does a sense that we might get lost in a system that we do not understand, and within which we have lost control over our lives.

A Citizen's Income would require no questions to be asked, would carry no fear that we might one day have to claim it (because everyone would receive it), would generate no fear that we would not understand the system (for everyone would understand it), and would offer us maximum control over our lives. A Citizen's Income would therefore generate no stigma. It would enable millions of people to dispense with means-tested benefits and would therefore reduce stigma in innumerable households; and if the particular Citizen's Income scheme implemented meant that some people remained on residual means-tested benefits, they would be on lower amounts of them and thus able to earn their way out of them quite quickly.

A Citizen's Income would reduce substantially the stigma suffered by individuals and thus by society as a whole, and because stigma drains our ability to function effectively, destroys relationships, prevents initiative, and results in ill health and particularly in depression, a reduction in stigma would have enormous benefits for individuals, communities, and the economy. If all a Citizen's Income did was to reduce stigma, it would be worth trying it for that reason alone.

## 38

# A Citizens Income is how people operate

Research by a group of sociologists on a housing estate in Exeter during the 1990s has proved that local communities ignore people bending means-tested benefits earnings rules up to a certain level of earned income, after which they are expected to declare their earned income or to come off benefits. [7] That Exeter community was effectively awarding itself a Citizen's Income, and we can realistically assume that other communities do the same.

It is rational for unemployed people not to declare casual earnings, and for employees on in-work means-tested benefits not to declare additional casual earnings. If benefits have to be recalculated then the claimant risks losing their benefits for several weeks while recalculation takes place, and later on they can receive demands for the repayment of overpaid benefits; and to declare additional earnings can cause large deductions in benefits, making it pointless to seek additional or casual earnings in the first place. This leaves someone with a difficult choice: either not to seek additional earnings, or to earn them and not to declare them.

It is therefore sensible for an occasional window cleaner who is on means-tested in-work or out-of-work benefits to wait until earnings have reached a high enough level to lift the family off means-tested benefits before contacting the benefits office. None of this is the window cleaner's fault. Neither in-work nor out-of-work means-tested benefits are designed for people who want to increase their household's disposable income by seeking additional employment.

Social policy is most effective if it reflects the morality of the community (providing the policy is not obviously immoral for other reasons), which suggests that we should relax the earnings rules on means-tested benefits, as that community in Exeter was doing. But that would create a new injustice, for the low earner still on benefits would then get a higher disposable income than the low earner not on benefits. The only solution to this dilemma is to give the same cash benefit to everyone – that is, to pay a Citizens Income – for only such a non-withdrawable payment will avoid such injustices.

The behaviour of people on that Exeter estate provides one of the strongest arguments ever for a Citizen's Income, for it begins with people's rational behaviour, it seeks a solution to the question posed to current regulations by that community's behaviour, it discovers an injustice in the initial solution, and it solves the injustice by finding a universal solution.

## 39

# A Citizen's Income would value unpaid work

Our income system is currently divided into two parts: earned income for those employed, and benefits for those without a job. The punitive regulations attached to means-tested benefits in the UK and elsewhere carry the double message that it is wrong to be receiving them and that it is equally wrong to undertake voluntary work or to follow a course of full-time study while receiving them. The system supports a hierarchy of esteem, with people in jobs regarding themselves, and being regarded by others, as morally superior to those not in jobs ( and however much we might not wish to recognise it, this is in fact how many of us feel).

A Citizen's Income would value unpaid work and paid work equally, because everybody would receive a Citizen's Income, however much paid work and however much unpaid work they were doing. Thus the old hierarchy of esteem would be replaced by a new one in which work was valued for its quality and for what it achieved. Unpaid educational and caring work, unpaid organisation of leisure activities, unpaid political and campaigning activity: all of this can be of enormous value to our society, our community, and ourselves. On the other hand, a great deal of paid work is destructive. In what respect (apart from providing an income for the industry's employees) can we place any positive value on the production of atomic warheads, the security measures to protect the factories that make them, or the anti-pollution activity that clears up after the manufacturing process? We would be no poorer if none of this activity occurred, so it does seem rather absurd that such activity contributes to the measurement of the 'Gross Domestic Product', whereas Mrs Jones coming to Dennis's school once a week to help him to learn to read does not appear in the calculation. People who make atomic warheads could spend their time building houses or teaching others in Dennis's class, but those activities do not provide an income, and those employees need to make a living. The hierarchy of esteem that values work that is paid more highly than work that is unpaid is one example among others of the ways in which money, once created, controls its creators: but if money is a human creation then we can change its behaviour if we choose to do so. We can therefore make it behave in such a way that it expresses the value of all good work, both paid and unpaid. A Citizen's Income would contribute to that process.

## 40

# A Citizen's Income would encourage voluntary activity

The care that parents give to their children, the care that people give to elderly parents, the time and energy that people put into youth clubs, scouts and guides, churches and tenants' associations, and young people's football clubs, the commitment that people bring to being local councillors and school governors, the voluntary work that people offer to schools and hospitals, the work of lifeboat men and of men and women in the special constabulary – all of this and more is unpaid, and it is essential to the welfare of individuals, families, and communities. Some of this work is done by people who earn their money elsewhere, and some by people who get their money from the State – but whoever does it, this work is both unpaid and essential, and it is often more important than work that is paid for. After all, which is more important: running a carers' and toddlers' group, or inventing and selling a new financial derivative?

Most unpaid voluntary activity is undertaken by the partners of earners, by part-time earners, and by retired earners, and not by people living in families in which no one is earning. The stigma of not earning a living is psychologically draining, which means that less energy is available for voluntary community activity. Because everyone would receive a Citizen's Income, and because receipt would involve no demeaning bureaucratic intrusion into the recipient's private affairs, no stigma would be experienced. A Citizen's Income would therefore give to everyone the psychological foundation required for purposeful community voluntary activity. (This is presumably at least one of the mechanisms behind the research finding that countries with higher levels of universal provision generate more social capital than other countries.) [8]

A Citizen's Income would value both paid and unpaid work, and so would increase the importance that our society ascribes to unpaid work in general and to voluntary community work in particular. We have seen that a Citizen's Income would provide a new widespread psychological basis for voluntary activity; and because a Citizen's Income would give to people in full-time employment, as well as to people with no employment, a greater ability to be employed part time or to be self-employed, time as well as energy could be released for voluntary community activity. So for a combination of reasons a Citizen's Income could mean that more people would participate in the gift economy than we might at first imagine.

41

## A Citizen's Income would encourage creative activity

South London, where we live, is full of artists, musicians, potters, sculptors, writers, and actors: and many of them just scrape by financially. Those who do eventually make significant amounts of money have frequently spent years making very little. Many of those who have created the literature, the philosophy, the poetry, the art, the music, and the drama that mean so much to us have, at least for parts of their lives, lived in poverty. And in South London, as elsewhere, much creative activity is undertaken for no money at all. Two of the parishes in which I have served have given birth to amazing community drama and to other artistic activity, and particularly to the annual Telegraph Hill Festival, still flourishing in New Cross, and the necessarily one-off Greenwich Passion Play in Greenwich Park on Good Friday 2000, with 800 in the cast. The number of voluntary hours that goes into this kind of creative activity is incalculable.

Some of us are fortunate enough to have jobs that leave us time for artistic, literary or musical pursuits, and time for organising arts festivals and passion plays: but not everyone is so fortunate. There will always be those so dedicated to their artistic vocation that they will almost starve in order to pursue it, but responsibility for dependents can make that way of life impossible for many.

With or without a Citizen's Income there will always be people who will pursue their vocation regardless, and a Citizen's Income would not solve all of the financial problems of artists, musicians, writers, and dramatists: but it would at least give to some people options currently closed to them. A Citizen's Income might enable musicians who would otherwise have to seek employment to continue full time in their quest for excellence; a Citizen's Income might enable someone to teach part time rather than full time and therefore have more time for composing; a Citizen's Income might give to a non-earning spouse the financial independence to pursue a course in sculpture; and a Citizen's Income might give to a group of artists sufficient money to survive on the sale of their work.

A Citizen's Income might be the catalyst for a flowering of new talent, and it might make possible the development of the talent of people who have the potential for greatness but who, without a Citizen's Income, would have to interrupt their pursuit of excellence in order to design birthday cards full time rather than give half the week to the creation of works of genius.

## 42

# A Citizen's Income would improve social cohesion

There is nothing wrong with difference. For a society to contain people of different ethnicities and different cultures can be creative and interesting. What is not helpful is that our society is divided by social class, by income inequality, and by wealth inequality. This results in unequal opportunities, particularly in terms of education, health, skills, physical environment, housing quality, and community and political participation. If one group in society possesses most of the opportunities, and another group possesses few, not only is social cohesion at risk, but the whole of society will be impoverished by the inability of some of its members to contribute as much as they would have been able to had they had the same opportunities as the fortunate.

The more aspects of the life of a society that its members can share, the more those members will feel that they belong to that society, the more they will want to participate in creating a good society, and the more they will want every member of that society to share in its opportunities. In the UK, the National Health Service is an essential institution in this respect, and Child Benefit is another (although the importance of its universality has not always been sufficiently recognised). Every citizen would receive an individual Citizen's Income, so this too would bind society together, enabling all of us to feel that we belong together.

A Citizen's Income would have another important social function that is not often recognised as such because the funding of a Citizen's Income is generally discussed separately from a Citizen's Income's social effects. Taxation is essential to the maintenance of a healthy society, so to pay income tax is to participate in the creation of such a society, is to feel that you are a member of such a society, and is a stimulus to political engagement: because if we pay income tax then we will have an interest in how that money is used by government. If we raise personal tax allowances then more low-earning households will be no longer be paying income tax, and this will disengage them from an important means of contributing to society. To pay a Citizen's Income to every citizen, and at the same time to reduce or abolish personal tax allowances, so that all or most earnings are taxed, would engage everyone earning an income in a joint project: the creation of a good society. The consequences for social cohesion and for political engagement could be considerable.

# C
# ADMINISTRATION

## 43

# A Citizen's Income would leave income tax calculation as the only income test

Most of us are subject to an income test: an income tax system. This is quite efficient – that is, it efficiently works out from our earnings and other income how much tax we should pay – largely because much of it happens automatically through a Pay As You Earn system, in which the employer deducts tax from earnings each month on the basis of a tax code and then passes the tax collected to the Government. The problem for people on means-tested benefits is that they suffer an inefficient means test, and employees who receive in-work means-tested benefits will often suffer two means tests: an income test attached to income tax and a means test attached to means-tested benefits. A Citizen's Income would require all or most earnings to be taxed, therefore most people would find themselves on an income tax income test, and few would suffer from a means test for benefits. Social integration and social justice would be enhanced and administrative costs would fall. After all, why do the same job twice?

If at the point of implementation of a Citizen's Income some means-tested benefits were retained, and households' means-tested benefits were reduced by their Citizen's Incomes in the same way as they are reduced by other income, then some people would still suffer two means tests: the more efficient income tax income test, and the less efficient means-tested benefits means test. Those households would be on far lower amounts of means-tested benefits, their marginal deduction rates would be lower than they are now, and they would therefore have both the ability and the desire to get off means-tested benefits by increasing their earned incomes.

Should the Citizen's Income be taxed? If it was taxed, and there was a tax allowance greater than the Citizen's Income, then those on low incomes would lose none of the benefit of their Citizen's Income (so there would be no harm in taxing it) and those paying tax at a higher rate would have their tax bill increased (because more of their income would be in the higher tax bracket). The arguments against taxing the Citizen's Income are that this would be administratively inefficient, that people paying tax at the higher rate are already paying more in tax than the amount of their Citizen's Income, and that to tax the Citizen's Income might make it less popular.

But whether or not the Citizen's Income is taxed, the principle remains the same. It is an automatic and unconditional payment that would be paid for through the operation of an efficient income test: the tax system.

## 44

# A Citizen's Income would require no case work

For every administrative saving, a civil servant is made redundant (or, at least, not recruited), and I would not wish redundancy on civil servants; but it does seem a waste of public money, and of civil servants' time, to investigate who is cohabiting with whom, and who is being paid by whom, and a waste of everybody's time to calculate small changes in benefits levels when claimants declare casual earnings.

The means-tested system, which includes in-work means-tested benefits, is now creaking in the UK and presumably elsewhere as well. The UK's system will continue to creak if Universal Credit really is rolled out to everyone on means-tested benefits, and it will creak even more now that Council Tax Support (a rebate on a local property tax) is calculated locally in relation to local rules. None of these systems is designed for a flexible labour market and a mobile society. If the nettle is not grasped soon then the system will make more and more mistakes, and will become more and more costly to run, and might eventually seize up, as Housing Benefit did in the mid-1980s.

New computers able to handle vast amounts of information at a speed thousands of times that of today's large computers are now being researched. These will make cheap administration of tax and benefits possible. But the case-by-case approach to benefits (including Universal Credit) will prevent effective computerisation. The casework approach means civil servants taking numerous decisions every time the smallest circumstance changes, and then transferring data to the computer. (This will still be true of Universal Credit, because automatic income reporting will only apply to employments for which Pay As You Earn tax is deducted.)

Only with a new start – only with a Citizen's Income – will the social security system reap the benefits of the next generation of computers. The UK's Child Benefit is already well computerised and is extremely cheap to administer (the Government has not means-tested it, contrary to popular belief) and there is no reason why a system to serve every citizen should not be like Child Benefit.

A Citizen's Income might still require a means-tested scheme to supplement it, but because many people currently on means-tested benefits would supplement their Citizen's Income with earnings rather than with means-tested benefits, there would be few people claiming means-tested benefits, and the casework approach would then be both appropriate and manageable, which it is not with the number of people relying on it today.

## 45

# A Citizen's Income would do away with work tests

To receive the UK's Jobseeker's Allowance you have to prove that you are seeking employment; so you fill in job application forms, and you go to interviews, and if you do not comply then sanctions are applied and you lose your Jobseeker's Allowance. But there are only so many job vacancies, with too many people chasing them, so employers receive hundreds of applications when a dozen from people genuinely interested in the job would have been enough. Is the overload sensible? Why not simply pay people benefits and leave the employment market to function as a market should?

The problem is that the right person for the job might be someone in the unemployment trap – that is, to take the job would leave them little better off, and if they would have fares to pay then they might end up worse off. Without a work test, and the associated sanctions, that potential employee would not apply. So to abandon the work test we would need to abolish the unemployment trap – and abolishing the unemployment trap would make the work test unnecessary, for the employment market would then work more like a true market, with supply and demand balancing each another more accurately. A Citizen's Income would reduce the unemployment trap, would remove work tests for millions of people, and would turn the employment market into something like a true market. There would be more sharing out of employment because people would demand employment with the number of hours that they wanted, and industry would provide it; more people who wanted employment would be able to find it; and most people would want employment because it would always be worth their while to earn an income.

If the work test were to be abolished then central government agencies would no longer need to collect job vacancies and force claimants to apply for them. In the UK, Local Authorities now have their own employment agencies that match local jobs to local people, and organise skills training where local people do not possess the skills necessary for jobs coming into the borough. This works, and it does not need a work test to make it work.

If we gave up on the work test then a whole raft of bureaucracy could be scrapped. If the cost of Jobcentre administration is added to the cost of administering Jobseeker's Allowance then the total cost is something like one third of the amount of Jobseeker's Allowance paid out. Such colossal administrative waste is unnecessary. With a Citizen's Income, it would stop.

46

# A Citizen's Income would make workfare and job guarantees unnecessary

'Workfare' is the idea that people should work for their benefits. All over Europe the unemployment rate refuses to drop, people without employment experience ever more virulent scapegoating, 'work tests' (benefits only being paid when claimants show evidence of looking for work) evolve into 'work experience' (claimants only paid their benefits when they work for companies for nothing), and we hear increasing talk of a 'job guarantee': jobs created by governments that claimants have to accept. This is the route that the French non-contributory benefit for unemployed people has taken, [1] and the UK's system is passing through similar stages.

The problem is that the employment market functions most efficiently when it is a genuine market: that is, when it is not interfered with, and supply and demand balance one another through the market-place constituted by job adverts and employment agencies. To run a workfare or job guarantee scheme skews the market and requires expenditure on administration, supervision, and policing, and it results in an alternative economy of the kind recently abandoned by Russia and Eastern Europe because of its chronic inefficiency. The present UK government is theoretically committed to the free market, but does not seem to have a problem with the skewed artificial market of 'work experience' and 'job guarantee'.

A Citizen's Income would make it always worthwhile for someone to seek earned income, and so would enable the employment market to function as a market. Why add to administrative costs with a job guarantee scheme when you could reduce them, and achieve better effects, by paying a Citizens Income?

Work tests, workfare, and job guarantees happen because we have a gut feeling that nobody should get something for nothing; but is not our real motive that we feel that nobody should get what we do not get? Would there still be such a psychological problem if *everybody* received a Citizen's Income? Would we not be happier with the idea that some people chose to live on a small income and not have a job if we got the same small income and had a job because we wanted one?

Whatever the psychological complexities, the administrative issue is a simple one. A job guarantee, and the insistence that benefits claimants should take the jobs offered, would only add to the administrative nightmare, and the nightmare would end if we all had a Citizen's Income.

## 47

# A Citizen's Income could be delivered easily

In the UK, 98% of households now have bank accounts [2] into which their Citizen's Incomes could be paid. A Citizen's Income pilot project in India, which required everyone in the pilot communities to have bank accounts after the first few weeks of the project, proved that it is not difficult to obtain almost 100% current account coverage in any country that chooses to implement a Citizen's Income. [3]

In the UK, 2% of households use Post Office Card Accounts. These are purely for the receipt of benefits, which can be drawn out at a Post Office on production of the card. Any country could establish such a mechanism. In the UK, mothers sometimes use these accounts to retain control over the family's Child Benefit. For the same reason, some individuals might wish their Citizen's Income to be paid into their Post Office Card Account rather than into a family's joint bank account.

In the UK, out-of-work means-tested benefits are paid fortnightly, in-work means-tested benefits are paid once every four weeks, and various other benefits have fortnightly or four-weekly payment cycles. Claimants can ask for weekly payments under certain circumstances. The new Universal Credit will be paid monthly. (This is because employers will report earnings to Her Majesty's Revenue and Customs monthly, HMRC will then report monthly to the Department for Work and Pensions, and the DWP will then pay the household's Universal Credit.) The reason for default payment periods is that contributory and means-tested benefits are complicated enough as it is, and giving claimants discretion over payment periods would complicate them even further. With a Citizen's Income this problem would not arise. Because every individual's Citizen's Income would be a fixed amount, everyone would be able to choose their own payment period. Even daily payments would be possible, which could help people living with addictions.

In the UK it is already possible for people without permanent addresses to receive benefits through a Post Office Card Account. It would be no problem for them to receive a Citizen's Income in the same way. Unlike other benefits, a Citizen's Income would never be reduced, so for the first time ever in the UK's history nobody would find themselves without an income, whatever their circumstances.

## 48

# A Citizen's Income could be established without imposing significant losses

If no additional public funds are available, then changes to the tax and benefits system will always generate gainers and losers. Does that matter?

A lot would depend on the changes in the existing system that would accompany any transition to a Citizen's Income. For instance, leaving existing means-tested benefits in place, and taking the new Citizen's Incomes into account when households' means-tested benefits are calculated could mean no losses for low-income households and only small losses for higher earners, whereas to abolish means-tested benefits on the implementation of a Citizen's Income could mean losses for some low-earning households. [4]

We can work out where some gains and losses would occur. The UK's current benefits system pays less to two people living together than it would pay to them in total if they were living apart. A Citizen's Income would not do that. If no additional public expenditure were to be available, then couples would gain and individuals not in couples would lose, though the losses would be smaller than some of those imposed by recent changes in means-tested benefits.

A larger Citizen's Income would require additional funding, so those taxpayers here whose Citizen's Incomes did not entirely compensate for additional tax payments would lose.

What gains and losses calculations cannot take into account is the way in which people's behaviour might change. With a means-tested benefits system, if benefits are reduced then it is difficult for a family to make up the difference by earning more, because earning more causes yet more of their benefits to be withdrawn. There might therefore be little behavioural change. With a Citizen's Income it would be easier to make up any loss by earning additional income, so for many people an initial loss would often result in additional employment. For some families, behavioural change might be substantial. For instance, families in which both parents are unemployed might come off means-tested benefits and rely on their Citizen's Incomes and on casual earnings. Small losses generated by a transition to a Citizen's Income would therefore be far less of a problem than losses caused by reductions in the levels of means-tested benefits. This is a significant reason for preferring Citizen's Incomes to means-tested benefits. It also means that small losses at the point of implementation might not be a problem, and that abolishing means-tested benefits completely could still be an option.

# 49

# A Citizen's Income would have predictable costs

No government can know how much it will spend each year on means-tested benefits, because it cannot predict how people's circumstances might change. The costs of universal benefits, such as the UK's Child Benefit, are of course far easier to predict.

Paying a Citizen's Income to every citizen would add to predictability. We can predict fairly accurately how many people will be born in any one year, and how many people will die, so we can predict quite accurately how much would be paid out if a Citizen's Income were to be established. Such greater predictability would enable governments to plan public expenditure with greater accuracy.

Because everyone would receive a Citizen's Income, everyone would understand how much it was costing, and would thus be in a position to discuss how large the Citizen's Income should be, unlike the current means-tested benefits system, the cost of which the public finds it difficult to evaluate. The tax rate required to fund a particular rise in Citizen's Incomes would still be a bit unpredictable, because tax receipts drop during a recession, grow as we come out of recession, and will drop generally as earned incomes become a smaller proportion of the proceeds of production. But with a Citizen's Income in place, a government would not suffer the double uncertainty of not knowing how much tax revenue would be brought in *and* not knowing how much would be spent on any and every benefit. Expenditure on any remaining residual means-tested benefits would remain uncertain, but a Citizen's Income would reduce the number of claims for means-tested benefits, and the amounts paid to each claimant would drop, so this area of unpredictability would reduce in importance.

With a Citizen's Income public opinion would be far better informed and would therefore have more influence on the levels of Citizen's Incomes than it has on the level of benefits at the moment; and because everyone would receive a Citizen's Income, the public would want to have more say, which would increase the democratic content of our life together. This would be very unlike the present system, where those who are paying and those who are receiving are largely different groups of people, creating incomprehension on both sides.

The greater predictability of costs that a Citizen's Income would offer is an argument that might appeal to ministries of finance, and in the UK to Her Majesty's Treasury, but it should also be an argument of interest to all of us.

50

# A Citizen's Income would have predictable effects

When a government changes a benefits regulation, it is not always obvious what the effects will be elsewhere in the system; and whether benefits and taxation are administered by the same government departments or by different ones, tax and benefits regulations rarely fit together, so changes to the tax system can have quite unpredictable effects on expenditure on means-tested benefits (including in-work benefits), and changes in benefits regulations can change labour market behaviour, and therefore tax receipts, in quite unpredictable ways. So not only are there good reasons for simplifying the system in order to create greater predictability, but there are also good reasons for creating institutional simplicity by establishing a single finance ministry rather than separate departments for tax and benefits. In the same way there are good reasons for integrating statistics on revenue foregone (through tax allowances that result in proportions of earned and unearned income not being taxed) with public expenditure figures, for otherwise the turning of tax allowances into cash payments would look like a large increase in public expenditure, whereas in fact it would be a small administrative change that would cost nothing.

Whether or not these sensible changes ever occur, a Citizen's Income would make the whole income maintenance system more predictable, because a change in the amount of a Citizen's Income would have totally predictable effects on expenditure on Citizen's Incomes, predictable effects on net disposable incomes, and predictable effects on other benefits. The only unpredictability would relate to changes in labour market behaviour, but such changes would be small and it would soon become possible to predict such changes for any given increase or decrease in the levels of Citizen's Incomes.

Whether or not Citizen's Incomes were taxable, the rise or fall of a Citizen's Income would have fairly predictable effects on money collected through taxes (though again, changing labour market activity could be a factor), and changes in the levels of the Citizen's Income would have predictable effects on expenditure on any remaining means-tested benefits, for means-tested benefits would take into account households' Citizen's Incomes and would rise or fall as Citizen's Incomes rose or fell. A rise in their Citizen's Incomes would encourage some people to replace their means-tested benefits with earnings, and a fall might have the opposite effect. Such labour market effects would, with time, become relatively easy to predict.

Any improvement in the predictability of the consequences of changes in tax and benefit levels and regulations is to be welcomed. A Citizen's Income would contribute substantially to such predictability.

## 51

# A Citizen's Income would experience an easy transition

It is not enough to recommend a new tax and benefits system. We also need to know how to get from where we are now to the system that we wish to arrive at.

This is not to say that transition must be easy; it must simply be possible, and not too difficult. In the UK, the transition from domestic rates to the Community Charge, and then to Council Tax, has been managed by local authorities – although the new localised Council Tax Support is not having an easy transition. It might eventually be possible to manage the transition to Universal Credit if it is taken slowly enough.

If means-tested benefits are abolished when a Citizen's Income is established, then transitional arrangements will be required to reduce the losses suffered by some low income families; but if means-tested benefits are left in place, and people's Citizen's Incomes are taken into account when means-tested benefits are calculated, then it will be easy to implement a Citizen's Income.

One way to implement a Citizen's Income would be to start paying it overnight, and to reduce tax allowances and benefits at the same time. Obviously there would need to be planning to ensure that every individual had a bank account, and that all other benefits were recalculated from the chosen date, but none of this would be difficult. The transition would be even easier if, instead of implementing a Citizen's Income for everyone at the same time, Citizen's Incomes were to be implemented for different age groups one after the other. We could create out of the new Single Tier State Pension a Citizen's Pension, starting with the very elderly and slowly reducing the age at which it was received; or we could start with a Citizen's Income for every 17-year-old and then let them keep it, so that after fifty years every adult would have a Citizen's Income. The easiest combination for implementation would probably be: 1) one age group at a time, and 2) leaving means-tested benefits in place and taking Citizen's Incomes into account when they are calculated in the same way as other income is taken into account. More research is required here, but because we can already describe at least one method by which we could implement a Citizen's Income, we can continue to discuss the idea and to hope that it will happen.

## 52

# A Citizen's Income would provide a new perspective on the tax system

A Citizen's Income would give a whole new look to tax and benefits systems. The reduction in tax allowances to pay for Citizen's Incomes would be a radical change to taxation, for tax would then be paid on most or all earned income, and such a change would make us ask a few questions about our tax system.

One of those questions would be whether we should keep a small tax allowance. The argument for keeping one is that tax authorities find it difficult to collect tax on small casual earnings. The disadvantage of keeping it is that even a small tax allowance means retaining a complex income tax structure. In the UK, employers receive a tax code for each employee, and they use this to calculate the amount of the employee's earnings to deduct and send to Her Majesty's Revenue and Customs (though to be fair, most of this is now done by computer). To abolish *all* tax allowances would be to simplify everything, because all an employer would then need to do would be to deduct tax at the published rate and send it to the tax authorities. Tax at higher rates could be collected from those earning above a specified figure after the annual tax return.

It might be objected that personal tax allowances recognise that a wage provides a subsistence income, and that only earnings above that level should be taxed, therefore we should not abolish personal tax allowances. My response to that is that a Citizen's Income is a better way of recognising our need for a subsistence income because everybody would benefit from it, whereas only those who earn at or above the personal tax allowance benefit from the whole of that allowance.

Another reform that might be considered at the same time would be the amalgamation of all personal taxation. In the UK, we still have two systems: Income Tax and National Insurance Contributions (NICs). NICs are an earnings tax (as was recently suggested in Parliament by a Conservative Member of Parliament), and the only reason for keeping them separate is so that the Chancellor of the Exchequer can tell us that he has not raised Income Tax rates when he has raised NICs. To amalgamate NICs with Income Tax would be an act of honesty that would reap administrative savings, and would at the same time give us a more progressive tax system.

Other countries will have their own personal tax complexities. The implementation of a Citizen's Income would provide a useful opportunity to sort them out.

## 53

# A Citizen's Income could be implemented in lots of different ways

A Citizen's Income is always an unconditional and non-withdrawable income for every individual as a right of citizenship; but there is an infinite number of possible Citizen's Income schemes, where by 'scheme' we mean the Citizen's Income, the age thresholds chosen, the Citizen's Income rates for each age group, and the changes made to existing tax and benefits systems. The number of possible Citizen's Income schemes is infinite.

For example, one scheme might abolish means-tested benefits when the Citizen's Income was implemented, but another scheme might retain them. If means-tested benefits were retained, then either means-tested benefits could be left exactly as they were, or a household's Citizen's Incomes could be taken into account when their means-tested benefits were calculated, thus reducing the amounts of means-tested benefits that households would receive. Each of these three options would generate different effects. To abolish means-tested benefits might generate losses at the point of implementation for households currently on high levels of means-tested benefits; to retain means-tested benefits in their current form would generate gains for everyone currently on means-tested benefits; and to retain means-tested benefits and to take households' Citizen's Incomes into account when they were calculated would mean that nobody on means-tested benefits would suffer losses, and that many households would no longer be on means-tested benefits. The different options would of course have different cost implications.

The virtue of a wide variety of different schemes being available, with different costs and different effects, is that there is always likely to be a Citizen's Income scheme that would satisfy contemporary financial, administrative, and political constraints. One scheme might be suitable in one country, and another might be more appropriate in another; and a scheme that might be appropriate at one point in time might not be appropriate ten years later. A country with no additional public funds available would need to select from among revenue neutral schemes, whereas a country with additional funds available would be able to choose from a broader field. Some countries might need to implement new conditional benefits alongside their Citizen's Income. But beware – if the Citizen's Income is made conditional in any way then it is no longer a Citizen's Income, and it won't deliver the many advantages that a Citizen's Income would offer.

Whatever the details of the Citizen's Income *scheme*, the definition of a Citizen's Income remains the same: it is an unconditional and non-withdrawable income for every individual. It is this that will make such a major difference to our economy and our society.

## 54

# A Citizen's Income could be optimised

To raise state pensions is popular but expensive; to raise contributory benefits is often irrelevant (because many of their recipients need means-tested supplements); and to raise means-tested benefits is electorally unpopular and digs people deeper into the unemployment and poverty traps. But to raise the Citizen's Income and raise the basic rate of income tax could cost nothing, would reinforce the many advantages of a Citizen's Income (in terms of creating enterprise, relieving the poverty trap, increasing social cohesion, etc.), and could be popular. At very high levels, a Citizen's Income would raise income tax rates to unacceptable levels and would be a disincentive to seek employment, but there are many potential levels of a Citizen's Income that would not do that, and it would be important to discover the ideal or optimal level of a Citizen's Income – the level that maximised the advantages but did not raise income tax to an unacceptable level.

At least with a Citizen's Income optimisation is possible. Nothing like it is possible with the current complex system. Every means-tested benefit comes with several variables: benefit levels for different age bands, earnings rules, savings rules, disregards, tapers, equivalisation (the ratio of the couple's rate to twice the individual rate) and so on. This complexity makes it impossible to state the optimal means-tested benefit. A Citizen's Income has a single set of variables: benefit levels for different age bands. Theoretical optimisation would be difficult because the effects of different levels of Citizen's Incomes on the labour market would be difficult to predict, but empirical optimisation would be a distinct possibility. An initially small Citizen's Income could be slowly raised, along with income tax rates, until it was clear that disadvantages of a rise were outweighing the advantages. The Citizen's Income and the tax rates could then be reduced and pegged.

There are of course other possibilities for the future, such as income tax rates on a sliding scale above a higher rate threshold (perfectly possible for computers to manage), additional taxes, and a Citizen's Income on a sliding scale according to age: but for the moment it would be enough to establish a Citizen's Income in order to test the principle. Optimisation could then follow. During that process the idea of a Citizen's Income must never be compromised, for were the payment to become in any way conditional or withdrawable then the payment would cease to be a Citizen's Income and its hard-won benefits would be lost.

## 55

# A Citizen's Income could be paid for in a variety of different ways

James Meade, the Nobel prize-winner in economics, recommended a Social Dividend. [5] This would be paid equally to every citizen, and it would be paid for out of a tax on industry rather than out of income tax, and so would recycle the profits of industry into disposable incomes. It would therefore increase consumption and contribute to the growth of the economy.

Alaska already has a Social Dividend. [6] Some of the royalties from oil extraction are allocated to an investment fund to provide an income when the oil runs out. The fund makes a profit, and a dividend is paid equally to every Alaskan citizen. The dividend is an annual payment that varies with the profits made by the permanent fund, and it is not a reliable weekly or monthly payment, so it is used for unusual purchases rather than for normal regular purchases. It is of interest that the Dividend has been shown to increase employment, but, because it is not a Citizen's Income, the amount that we can learn from it will be limited. What is clear is that the social dividend approach could be used to part fund a more regular Citizen's Income. The higher the proportion of such funding, the more pronounced would be the Citizen's Income's effect on the growth of the economy.

A further possibility is to fund a national or Europe-wide Citizen's Income out of national or European carbon taxes. The carbon taxation and Citizen's Income debates must be kept separate from each other, because they are separate issues; but if in both cases the advantages were to outweigh the disadvantages, then there would be no harm in using carbon taxes to pay for a European Citizen's Income. The package would improve economic efficiency, benefit European society, contribute to European social cohesion, and benefit the environment.

Reductions in personal tax allowances and of means-tested and other benefits could fund a Citizen's Income in the short term, and there are several ways of funding a Citizen's Income in the longer term, so there is every reason to continue to discuss the feasibility and desirability of a Citizen's Income.

# 56

## A Citizen's Income would reduce benefits fraud

When I worked in Brixton's Supplementary Benefit office it horrified me that so much time and energy was spent tracking down fraud and prosecuting claimants. People who were earning money as stall-holders, roofers, or early-morning cleaners were prosecuted for claiming means-tested benefits while earning an income; people were prosecuted for not declaring that they were living together as husband and wife, or for taking a lodger and not declaring the income. All they were trying to do was to provide for their families. To have declared their earnings would have resulted in substantial reductions in benefits. What they were doing was illegal, and it was unjust in relation to those claimants who did declare their occasional earned incomes, but it was understandable.

We prosecuted separated fathers for not paying maintenance for their children, even though this was counter-productive. Declared maintenance payments were deducted from the mother's means-tested benefits, and prosecution usually caused the father's covert financial help to stop. Nobody benefited from any of this.

In all of these cases, the problem was not people's desire to improve the financial position of their families. The problem was a means-tested benefits system that deducted substantial amounts of benefits when other income increased. Why get up early to help out on a market stall on Saturdays if the earnings will make almost no difference to the family's disposable income, and if declaring the inevitably varying income would cause benefits to be endlessly stopped, recalculated, and restarted? My experience of all of this was nearly forty years ago, but the situation is still much the same. The main difference is that television companies now make money out of exposing benefits fraud.

A Citizen's Income would minimise fraud because there would be nothing to be fraudulent about. People could live with who they wished without affecting their Citizen's Income; they could earn money in a wide variety of different ways without affecting their Citizen's Income; and they could support their separated children without affecting either the children's or their mother's Citizen's Incomes. Much administrative effort, police officers' time, and law court resources would be saved. There is quite enough criminality without adding totally unnecessary fraud prosecutions to the already difficult relationships that many communities experience with the police, officials, and the courts.

Regulations that turn into crimes what most members of a normal community would regard as sensible behaviour sap the morale of the community and bring the law into disrepute. A Citizen's Income has no such regulations attached to it, and would substantially reduce the volume of criminality.

# 57

# A Citizen's Income would reduce administrative errors

Wherever a decision has to be made, error will always be a possibility. The more complex a system is, the greater will be the number of decisions that have to be made, and therefore the greater the likelihood of error.

Genuinely universal and unconditional benefits generate almost no errors. Take for example the UK's Child Benefit. This starts when a child is born and it ends when they are 16 years old, or when they are 20 years old if they remain in approved full-time education or training. The only decisions that have to be made relate to how many children there are in the family (the rate for the first child is different from the rate for subsequent children), and who the responsible parent is. Rarely will the responsible parent change. Annual uprating is computerised. Very few errors occur.

Social insurance or contributory benefits generate more errors, but still not many. Payment generally starts when a contingency occurs (someone reaches the state retirement age, or they sign on as unemployed, or they present a medical certificate to say that they are ill). Payment ceases when the contingency no longer applies (the claimant is no longer sick or unemployed), and the benefits often run out anyway after a defined period. Household constitution might or might not affect the amount of benefit paid, and money earned while the contingency is in place might or might not affect the amount of benefit payable. If either of these factors do apply then complexity will be the result, decisions will need to be made, any decision arrived at will need to be formulated into data to enter into a computer, and errors might occur.

With means-tested benefits, error is ubiquitous. Numerous changes of circumstances – occasional earnings, household changes, changes in the earnings of other household members – need to be reported, recorded, and turned into data to enter into a computer. If an underpayment is later discovered then the claimant can get a nice surprise. If an overpayment is discovered then repayment is usually demanded, anxiety is the result, and the Government suffers yet more administrative cost as it attempts to recover the debt.

A Citizen's Income would be the simplest possible benefit. It would start at birth, and as the citizen's age changed their Citizen's Income would adjust automatically. While someone was a child a decision would need to be made as to who was their responsible parent, but that is the only decision that would ever have to be made. The error rate would be close to zero.

## 58

# A Citizen's Income would reduce the mythology in the system

In the UK, the amount of 'National Insurance' Basic State Pension that someone receives is a political decision and bears only a loose relationship to the amounts of 'National Insurance Contributions' paid in. Neither is Contributory Unemployment Benefit an insurance benefit. The Government can invent new conditions, reduce the benefit, or even withhold it. (The situation is different in Germany and a number of other countries, where employees' and employers' contributions build a fund out of which unemployment benefits are paid.) The UK's 'contributory principle' is a myth that enables the Government to extract an earnings tax that it calls 'National Insurance Contributions' while being able to publish low Income Tax rates, but also usefully enables pensioners and other recipients to feel that they have earned their payout.

When I was administering means-tested benefits, Supplementary Benefit was rarely supplementary to anything; today, Working Tax Credits are not tax credits (they are not administered through the tax system), and the new Universal Credit is neither universal nor a credit. (Other countries have problems too – means-tested child benefit in Australia is for some reason called 'Family Tax Benefit'.)

Means-tested benefits are apparently an 'entitlement', [7] but they can be reduced if a claimant's spouse's earnings rise, and for a variety of other reasons. We are told that means-testing 'targets' money on those who need it most: but to 'target' like this is a blunt instrument [8] that separates the targeted from the rest of society, which creates stigma and reduces take-up. [9] The only effective targeting is universal benefits, for these are the most effective at getting money to where it is needed.

Why is the UK so uniquely wedded to problematic language? I don't know. But what I do know is that a Citizen's Income would have none of these problems. It would be an income for citizens; it would be truly an entitlement; and it would target money where it was most needed.

The biggest myth of all is the UK's published public expenditure figure. This leaves out the revenue foregone through tax not being paid on earnings up to the personal tax allowance. If personal tax allowances were turned into cash payments of the same value, and then tax was levied on all earned income, neither the citizen nor the government would see any difference in their disposable income: but the public expenditure figure would rise. This is ridiculous. Tax revenue foregone is public expenditure, and it is time that it was measured as such.

# 59

## A Citizen's Income would be simplicity itself

When I worked in the Supplementary Benefit office in Brixton, the code of regulations for means-tested benefits filled a bookshelf. The claimants didn't understand the regulations, and neither did we. The complexity, combined with the stigma attached to the system, led to take-up being well under 100%, and to local authority campaigns to persuade people to claim their entitlements. The error rate was astronomical, a situation made worse by the mobility of both Brixton's population and the office's staff ( after two years I was in the 50% of the staff that had been there the longest). Any system that combines means-tested benefits with contributory benefits, and that constantly adapts to new contexts and changing political pressures, will suffer from increasing complexity. But at least in the UK we have a single national benefits system. The United States too has a benefits system that is partly based on contributory benefits and partly on means-tested benefits, but the means-tested system is different from state to state, so that moving across a state boundary can mean getting to know a different benefits system. The possibilities for complexity are endless. By localising Council Tax Support, the UK is heading in the same direction.

The solution is a system with no regulations, because only then will there be nothing to make complicated. A Citizen's Income would be as close to such a system as it is possible to get. The only regulations required would be rules to determine who should receive Citizen's Incomes, rules to determine who should receive Child Citizen's Incomes (an issue of which the UK already has some experience in relation to Child Benefit), and rules to determine who should manage the Citizen's Incomes of people who cannot manage them themselves (this is another issue of which the UK has experience in other areas). Such regulations would not complicate the Citizen's Income itself, which would remain totally without regulation, because it is an unconditional, non-withdrawable and automatic income for every individual citizen. The extreme simplicity of a Citizen's Income would result in the simplest possible administration, in 100% take-up, and in increasing demand for simplicity in other areas of social policy.

A constantly changing context does not need a system designed for today's context, because it would be quickly out of date, it would need to be changed, and it would suffer from increasing complexity. What is required is a system that will suit any context, and only a radically simple system will be able to do that.

## 60

# A Citizen's Income would be easy to understand

When twenty years ago the UK charity Age Concern commissioned research into what the public's attitude might be to a Citizen's Income, [10] a major conclusion was that people did not understand the current benefits system, let alone the implications of changing it. The system is not transparent: that is, it is not immediately comprehensible. This is not surprising, as the UK's benefits system has evolved over five centuries, and during the past sixty years has been constantly tinkered with. Quite often a claimant will not even understand the parts of the system to which they relate, let alone the parts of which they have no direct experience. If legislators and the public do not understand a system then they will not be comfortable discussing it in case their ignorance is revealed: and nobody wants to admit that they don't understand something important.

A Citizen's Income, on the other hand, could not be more transparent. The regulations governing its administration would be minimal, and its universal nature and unconditionality would mean that everybody would receive it and everybody would understand it.

It might seem strange that the idea is not at the moment universally understood, but this is in fact perfectly comprehensible. When a Citizen's Income is explained to somebody who has not previously heard of the idea, they try to put it into some existing category (such as means-tested benefits, or a National Minimum Wage), which confuses both them and their educator. Comparison with existing universal benefits, such as the UK's Child Benefit and NHS, can help the penny to drop, but sometimes it is extremely difficult to get across the message that a Citizen's Income would be totally without conditions. We find it hard to imagine any institution giving something to everybody without strings attached.

But once we had a Citizen's Income it would be entirely transparent, for we would experience the unconditionality of it, and our Citizen's Income would then begin to change the shape of the categories that we use to evaluate social policy options. There would no longer be any division between those who understood the benefits system (or, at least, thought they did) and those who did not (although understanding any remaining means-tested benefits would remain a challenge). There would be a transparency the like of which we have never experienced before, and one that we might then wish to see duplicated in other areas of government activity.

# D
# POLITICS

## 61

# A Citizen's Income would contribute to a definition of citizenship

Where there is already a clear definition of citizenship, a Citizen's Income would be paid to every citizen, but in some countries the situation is rather less clear. In the UK, immigrants can pay a fee, pass an exam, and become 'citizens', and UK passports usually say 'British Citizen', but the UK has no clear definition of citizenship. The government can decide who has a right to live in the United Kingdom and for how long, sometimes on an ad hoc basis; and the fact that some people have a right to live here, but need to apply to become citizens, is evidence that the UK's definition of citizenship is somewhat fuzzy. It would therefore not be entirely clear who should receive a Citizen's Income. If the precedent of Child Benefit were to be followed, then anyone with a right to live in the UK, and for whom the UK was their main home, would receive a Citizen's Income. (A decision would need to be taken as to whether to pay a Citizen's Income to British citizens living abroad.) A waiting period between arriving in the UK and receiving a Citizen's Income could replicate the waiting period before receiving Child Benefit. This might prevent the Citizen's Income getting mixed up in the somewhat rancorous debate about the level of immigration and the number of migrants claiming benefits in the UK (a somewhat ill-informed debate. There are more Britons receiving unemployment benefit in other EU states than there are citizens of other EU states receiving benefits in the UK.)[1] Where other countries pay a Child Benefit similar to the UK's, a reciprocal agreement enables migrants in either direction to avoid a waiting period. Similar reciprocal agreements could be agreed between countries that pay Citizen's Incomes. (Once one country pays a Citizen's Income, others might well follow in order to reap the same benefits and maintain economic competitiveness, so the possibility of reciprocal agreements would need to be addressed fairly quickly.)

Not only would decisions about citizenship determine who should receive a Citizen's Income, but receipt of a Citizen's Income would deepen the definition of citizenship. In most countries, legal citizenship confers political and social rights, at least in theory. Rarely are strictly economic rights conferred. A Citizen's Income would constitute an economic citizenship alongside our legal, social, and political citizenships. This could only be good for the cohesion of a nation state.

# 62

# A Citizen's Income would generate a deeper consciousness of citizenship

A Citizen's Income would be paid to citizens, so citizenship relates to a Citizen's Income's administration; but it also relates to a Citizen's Income as a political issue.

For a nation state to function as a coherent political unit, an essential requirement is that every member of its society should feel themselves to be a citizen of that state – emotionally as well as theoretically. In many countries the national flag and public holidays marking important anniversaries contribute to a sense of shared citizenship. In the UK, the monarchy contributes both to a sense of shared citizenship and ambiguity over the issue, for we are still strictly speaking subjects of a monarch who appoints a government, rather than citizens who elect one.

Shared institutions can contribute to a sense of shared citizenship, particularly where other factors make citizenship problematic. Many countries' external and internal borders are the products of difficult histories, and the resulting pressures for devolutions and annexations can be difficult for national and regional governments to handle. No social institution can solve the resulting political pressures entirely, but social institutions that encourage a shared sense of citizenship can help such pressures to be managed slowly and rationally rather than rapidly and explosively. In the UK, it is interesting how significant the possibility of Scotland losing the British Broadcasting Corporation became in the debate leading up to the referendum on Scottish independence. The BBC is funded by everyone resident in the UK who wishes to access its television output, and everyone, both within the UK and around the world, can access its radio and website outputs for free. It would be difficult to identify a social institution that contributes more creatively to the binding together of the UK's citizens, and also of citizens of different nations, both within the UK and around the world.

Citizenship has two aspects: a sense of shared citizenship, and a sense of oneself as an individual citizen with rights and responsibilities. They are equally important, and a Citizen's Income would facilitate both. A Citizen's Income would be a social institution that would bind together every citizen into a cohesive society; and it would provide every individual with an income as a right, and with a greater ability to contribute to society through employment, through caring for one's family, and through community activity.

What better way to affirm everyone's citizenship than by giving everyone a small income? And what better way to create a nation state than for a Citizen's Income to reinforce both the shared and individual aspects of citizenship?

## 63

# A Citizen's Income would unite workers of all kinds

In 1992, twelve countries' governments signed the Maastricht Treaty which turned the European Economic Community into the European Union. The UK persuaded the EU's member states to amend the treaty's Social Chapter so that it referred to 'workers' rather than to 'citizens', and then negotiated an opt-out. By 'workers' the chapter did not mean 'anybody doing any kind of work: paid, voluntary, caring, or otherwise': it meant employees and the self-employed. So for the purposes of this reason only, 'worker' means 'paid worker'.

In most countries, not every worker is a citizen and not every citizen is a worker. There are four groups: nonworker-noncitizens; worker-noncitizens; worker-citizens; and nonworker-citizens. Usually the tax system is for workers and the benefits system for the nonworkers. In the UK the division is made clearer by the two groups being dealt with by different government departments: Her Majesty's Revenue and Customs for workers, and the Department for Work and Pensions for the rest, which is somewhat ironic. The division is then rendered less clear by many workers receiving means-tested in-work benefits to top up their low wages.

The fracture between workers and nonworkers is perpetuated by the economic and political power of workers exercised through trades unions as well as by governments and businesses. Political parties are often funded by trades unions or by companies, so they serve workers' interests and tend to neglect the rest. It is workers who pay taxes and who therefore expect more of a say than nonworkers – unless those nonworkers belong to the growing number of elderly people, who through their voting power can maintain the level of state pensions. As technology automates more and more jobs, those who are not already workers are going to be left further behind as the major political parties pursue the votes of workers who will, after all, still constitute the majority of a population.

A Citizen's Income would begin to repair the fracture by enabling people to escape from the unemployment trap, become workers, and therefore participate in politics in ways in which workers often do and nonworkers often do not; and a Citizen's Income, by treating workers and nonworkers in the same way, would dissolve the boundary between them and enable those unable to become workers to feel themselves responsible for the state of the nation. Then if we declared all legal residents to be citizens we would unite all workers and nonworkers in the 'citizen' category, 'workers' would mean workers of all kinds – as it should – and social cohesion would be considerably enhanced.

## 64

# A Citizen's Income would help to solve the problem of housing costs

Housing costs vary. This simple fact suggests that a Citizen's Income would not help to solve the problem of high housing costs. However, although it would not be a complete solution to the problems of housing costs and housing shortages, it would make contributions to the solution of both.

For someone currently on means-tested benefits, additional earnings can make little difference to disposable income. If the family's rent rises, or mortgage payments increase, or a change of job requires a move to an area with higher housing costs, then additional earnings will often make little difference to disposable income, and additional means-tested benefits will be the only answer. Because for so many families higher housing costs automatically generate higher means-tested benefits, landlords have an incentive to increase rents for families on means-tested benefits, and will often seek such families as tenants. The situation becomes a vicious circle; and just as the employment disincentives in the benefits system can require sanctions to encourage people into employment, so benefit caps and accommodation size penalties (such as the UK's 'bedroom tax') are used to encourage families to move to smaller accommodation (if there is any).

If a Citizen's Income were to replace most or all of means-tested benefits, then families would more easily earn their way into higher disposable incomes, and any families still on means-tested benefits could more easily come off them. For families now off means-tested benefits, housing sanctions would no longer exist. For their landlords, no longer would increases in rent be met by increases in means-tested benefits, so upward pressure on rents would reduce; and because families would need to find their rents out of their own earned incomes, downward pressure on rents would increase. The housing market would more closely resemble a genuine market, with the price mechanism matching supply and demand. (A quite different interference in a country's housing market from investors from abroad would require a solution of its own.)

One of the problems attached to means-tested benefits is that it is often financially beneficial for members of couples to live apart, and for individuals not to move in together. The individual basis of a Citizen's Income would provide no incentive for couples to split up, and because it would leave economies of scale with the couple, rather than extracting them for the government, as means-tested benefits do, it would not discourage the formation of households. Both of these processes would reduce the pressure on the existing housing stock, would reduce the need for additional housing, and, by reducing demand, would reduce rents and house prices.

# 65

# A Citizen's Income would lead to additional universal benefits

Citizen's Income is a simple idea, but its introduction would result in some complex issues that would need to be tackled: not because there is anything wrong with a Citizen's Income, but because there are problems with the way in which we organise other benefits.

Take the example of school meals in the UK. These are received free by families on means-tested benefits; but if a Citizen's Income were to enable most families to do without means-tested benefits, then they might lose free school meals and end up worse off. The problem with free school meals only being received by families on means-tested benefits is that they dig those families deeper into the unemployment trap or poverty trap. The solution is to provide a free school meal for every child. This is now being tried. Every child in the first three years of primary school now receives a free school meal, which improves nutrition and therefore learning. [2] Now all that is required is to extend free school meals to every child. There would then be no problem left to be solved if a Citizen's Income were to be introduced.

The argument that some families do not need free school meals is as flawed as the argument that some families do not need Citizen's Incomes. Wealthier families pay more in tax than their children's school meals cost, and they would be paying more in tax than their Citizen's Incomes would cost. Providing a benefit or a meal for everyone is administratively efficient and promotes an integrated society rather than a divided one. It is therefore sensible to provide both universal free school meals and a universal Citizen's Income, and there is no reason not to.

In general, except where free provision might encourage abuse, there is a good case for free provision (for instance, of dental check-ups). Where overuse is more of a possibility (for instance, with the supply of spectacles), a small payment element might be appropriate; and where the issue lies between these points (for instance, with medicines), subsidies and season tickets are appropriate.

Whatever the future of benefits in kind, such as free school meals, one of the advantages of a Citizen's Income would be that it would force us to re-examine them and to go back to first principles. And what better starting point than the Citizen's Income principle: that universal provision is administratively efficient, reduces the debilitating effects of the poverty and unemployment traps, offers the possibility of 100% take-up, reduces stigma, and contributes to the creation of a cohesive society.

# 66

## A Citizen's Income has precedents

Precedents are a good reason for doing something, because if something has worked before then something like it might work now; and a precedent means that an idea might be given the benefit of the doubt until it is proved that it won't work, and this might oil the wheels of the political process.

In the UK, the National Health Service and state-provided education, which are free at the point of use, are precedents for universal benefits. They are more efficient than insurance-based or voucher-based systems, and they are electorally popular. The closest precedent to a Citizen's Income in the UK is Child Benefit, paid unconditionally for every child. (It is still an unconditional benefit. A tax on children is now levied on the incomes of higher rate taxpayers who live in households that receive Child Benefit, but that is a different matter.) Child Benefit is efficient, it does not contribute to the poverty and unemployment traps, it targets benefit where it is most needed, those who do not need it pay more in Income Tax than they receive in Child Benefit, it is a constant source of income when people move in and out of employment, and take-up was 100% until women in households containing a higher rate taxpayer started to withdraw their claims in order to avoid domestic disharmony. (Child Benefit is taken into account in the calculation of means-tested benefits, and therefore does not directly benefit people on means-tested benefits: but that is the fault of those benefits and not of Child Benefit. In the same way, if means-tested benefits were retained, a household's Citizen's Incomes would be taken into account in the calculation of any remaining means-tested benefits. What matters is that Child Benefit does not stop when someone's earned income rises. The same would be true of someone's Citizen's Income).

The precedent of Child Benefit is the most important for our purposes, and it might be that the Citizen's Income debate will be important for the future of Child Benefit. Some people think that by means-testing Child Benefit they would benefit the poorest members of society. They would not.

New Zealand operates a universal state pension – a Citizen's Income – so New Zealand can regard that as a precedent; the UK's new Single Tier State Pension will be almost a universal benefit and will therefore function as something close to a precedent; and the UK's Winter Fuel Allowance for pensioners is already a precedent. They are all preferable to means-tested alternatives. We need all of these precedents, and above all we need a Citizen's Income.

## 67

# A Citizen's Income would be in continuity with the Beveridge Report

The intention of the UK's Beveridge Report of 1942, and of the legislation that followed, was to tackle the evil of 'want' by reforming a patchwork of private and public benefits into a system of National Insurance benefits backed up by a means-tested National Assistance. The system has served well, and it is not my task here to criticise Beveridge (although he ought to have known that the assumptions that he made about family structure, the dependence of women, and the stability of the labour market were less than accurate at the time at which he wrote his report). My task here is to note that we are still trying to solve the problem of want, and that in a changing world Beveridge's solution is not necessarily the one that we need.

Beveridge's chief concern was not in fact with 'want', but with 'idleness'. Since his student days he had been a passionate advocate of full employment, and had had a horror of 'idleness', both his own and everyone else's. [3] Beveridge thought that poverty could be cured by ensuring that every male had full-time paid employment, and his benefits system assumed that this dream of full employment would come true (as it did on the whole during the 1950s and 1960s). Paid employment is now, as it was then, a way out of poverty, and to achieve this end we need to seek out appropriate social policy, as Beveridge did. The benefits system that has evolved from Beveridge's National Insurance and National Assistance benefits has embroiled far too many people in benefits-induced disincentives both in and out of work. Today we shall tackle want more effectively than Beveridge did if we make it easier for people to increase their disposable income and thus earn their way out of poverty. Beveridge had been converted to unconditional Family Allowances (which later became Child Benefit), and if he had been writing today, with our more flexible labour market and family structures in mind, he might have recommended a Citizen's Income.

Beveridge's horror of idleness led him to develop a benefits system that contained a work test. Again, if he had been writing today, then that same horror of idleness might have led him to ask what kind of benefits system would be the most likely to encourage employment. The answer is: a system that would deliver the fewest disincentives. A Citizen's Income – without a work test – would do that. Beveridge would have been listening.

68

# A Citizen's Income scheme could be revenue neutral

In 1982, I was a curate in the parish in which stood the headquarters of the UK Government's Department of Health and Social Security. The Department invited me to their summer school, a stimulating gathering of staff members, academics, and others. The overall aim was to debate policy options that would be revenue neutral, that is, that would require no additional public expenditure. We are still in the same situation, both in the UK and around the world. Unless there are overwhelming political reasons for spending more money, the presupposition is that public expenditure will go down, not up, and that, in order to be discussed, new social policies will need to be revenue neutral.

A Citizen's Income was debated at that summer school partly because it could be introduced in a revenue neutral fashion. Obviously we can think of Citizen's Income schemes that would cost a great deal, but in today's circumstances these can only be discussed as longer term options unless savings can be made elsewhere. We can also design Citizen's Income schemes that could be paid for by reducing tax allowances and adjusting income tax rates and means-tested and other benefits. It is only such revenue-neutral schemes that we consider in this book.

Here we need to be clear what we mean by 'revenue neutral'. A Citizen's Income scheme can still be termed revenue neutral if it requires income tax rates to be raised and tax allowances to fall, but not if it requires additional revenue from outside the income tax system. However, if income tax rates are to be raised, then an additional constraint will apply. If the scheme as a whole were to impose losses on low-earning households, then it would not be politically viable or fair even if it was revenue neutral.

So what we require is a Citizen's Income scheme that requires no additional funding from outside the benefits and income tax systems, and that imposes no losses on low income households. Research has shown that such a scheme is not possible if means-tested benefits are abolished entirely. However, such a scheme is possible if means-tested benefits are retained and individuals' Citizen's Incomes are taken into account when households' means-tested benefits are calculated. We only require one such scheme, and one such scheme exists. [4] In the longer term, we would hope for a higher Citizen's Income and an end to means-tested benefits. In the meantime, the implementation of the entirely feasible scheme discussed here will be enough to be getting on with.

## 69

# A Citizen's Income would target money where it is needed

Governments are expected to keep tax rates low at the same time as protecting the poor from poverty. Governments are particularly expected to protect children, older people, and those with disabilities. So the 'targeting' of scarce resources on those sections of the population that most need help is going to be attractive.

The problem is that to target 'the poor' requires that we define 'the poor'. If we then target money on the poor, some of them will cease to be poor. But those who cease to be poor will then cease to receive the public expenditure that had previously been targeted on them, so they will remain poor or they will again become poor. This makes it difficult for people to cease to be poor, so 'targeting' like this will never reduce the number of people in poverty. This is not the intention, as nobody in their right mind would purposely create a group of poor people who would find it difficult to cease to be poor, but the targeting of means-tested benefits, particularly on adults of working age, has precisely that effect. No social policy ever comes without some ill effects, but here we have a policy with large and well known ill effects, and yet we do nothing about it.

A Citizen's Income does not look like good targeting, but it would in fact be precisely the targeting that we need. A Citizen's Income would ensure that money went to the poorest members of society (because it would go to everybody); everyone would receive a Citizen's Income, so it would achieve widespread appeal and would therefore maintain its value; [5] there would be no stigma attached to it, so payments would be welcomed; administration would be simple, so no one would be put off receiving their Citizen's Income; and it would be paid for out of income taxation, so wealthier people would pay more in tax then they would receive in Citizen's Income. The Citizen's Income would not cease when someone ceased to be poor, so it would have none of the ill effects that some other targeting exhibits. A Citizen's Income would reduce the number of poor people and would therefore be very good targeting.

There is nothing wrong with targeting, but there is a lot wrong with the way that we do it today. A Citizen's Income would do it better.

# 70

# A Citizen's Income would increase social morale and stability

In 1991, when Norman Lamont was the UK's Chancellor of the Exchequer, he offered the opinion that unemployment was a price that was 'well worth paying'[6] for low inflation. This is a minority view among politicians, because most of them know that unemployment is bad for individuals and bad for society. To seek a job and not find one depresses morale and increases anxiety, and a high unemployment rate increases the anxiety experienced by people in employment, and creates ill health and thus increased healthcare costs. In communities where large numbers of people are unemployed, shops and other businesses go out of business, and the local economy enters a downward spiral from which it finds it difficult to recover. Few people in developed countries will starve, and unemployed people are rarely well organised, so social chaos will be rare, but blighted lives and the deterioration of communities are sufficient causes for concern.

A Citizen's Income would be politically attractive because its universality would improve social cohesion, because it would alleviate the poverty and unemployment traps and therefore encourage people into employment, and because it would enable the employment market to become more diverse and more flexible and therefore to generate employment for a larger number of people. An important additional effect of the more flexible employment market that a Citizen's Income would deliver would be to make it more difficult to define 'unemployment' and 'the unemployed'. There would still be poverty, poverty would still be measured, and it would remain a cause for concern if too many families were living on an income below 60% of mean earnings. But the disappearance of meaningful unemployment figures would mean that poverty would be seen to be the important issue that it is, and we might try harder to do something about it.

A Citizen's Income would improve many people's ability to find or create employment and would therefore improve people's morale and would provide people with the motivation to spend time and energy on their families and communities (for it is those in employment who tend to do this, rather than those who are not). A Citizen's Income would eradicate 'the unemployed' as a category, would draw attention to poverty, and would thus help to eradicate it. None of this would happen overnight, but a Citizen's Income would create the conditions for it happening, and would thus help to maintain social order. For this reason alone a Citizen's Income should be seriously considered.

## 71

# A Citizen's Income could be usefully Europe-wide

The European Union's principle of subsidiarity – that decisions and activity should be as local as possible – suggests that the EU's task is to support national social security systems, and where necessary to provide coordination, but the complexity involved in any relationship between different countries' welfare systems means that is difficult to achieve. In his 1992 Institute for Fiscal Studies annual lecture, Professor Tony Atkinson suggested that because we now have a free market in labour, employees who know that tax rates are lower in other member states will be able to pressurise their own governments to reduce tax rates. This led Professor Atkinson to suggest EU intervention to ensure the maintenance of current levels of welfare provision. James Meade has similarly suggested that because harmonisation of existing schemes would be difficult, the EU should establish a Citizen's Income, and then leave individual member states free to experiment with their own distinctive social security schemes. [7] This option would suit a free market in labour, would encourage a new and more diverse full employment, would involve a minimal bureaucracy, would preserve national self-determination in relation to social security provision, would encourage national experiment, and would result in an economy more consistent across Europe, and one less likely to create social exclusion or regional marginalisation.

Without common welfare benefits, countries in an economic community committed to free markets in goods, services and labour will seek bilateral or multilateral agreements in order to coordinate their existing systems (such as the provision of free healthcare on the presentation of the prescribed form issued in any of the member countries, or agreements between countries over the payment of child benefits). Such bilateral or multilateral agreements cannot create consistency, because national systems remain different; and because any part of a country's system is intertwined with other parts of it, it is very difficult for any country to align any part of its own complex system with any part of another country's complex system. Another problem with bilateral and multilateral agreements is that they constrain a country's ability to alter its benefits and tax systems, so national autonomy and initiative might be lost, and the subsidiarity principle might be compromised. Such agreements therefore offer the worst of all worlds: neither autonomy nor consistency. A Europe-wide Citizen's Income would offer the best of all worlds: both consistency across Europe, and national autonomy and initiative.

# 72

# A Citizen's Income would promote social inclusion in Europe

We now take for granted the free movement of citizens and goods between different parts of the European Union; so it is in a European context that we should discuss social exclusion, and not just in a national one.

People on low incomes have less choice than others: about where they live, about their housing tenure, about their children's schooling, about their leisure activities, and about much more besides. Where means-testing is an important part of the social security system, people who cannot earn much are excluded from creating additional wealth for themselves and for their families.

Sometimes social exclusion is invisible (for instance, where poorer people live in a generally wealthy community), and sometimes an area has less social exclusion than one might think (for instance, where an active informal economy enables people to take part in the economic and social life of their communities). In different regions poverty is different. Material circumstances that in Liverpool would create social exclusion might not do so in rural Portugal. In some places the poverty is deep enough for the presence of social exclusion to be beyond doubt and to be without obvious solution, and in such places an 'underclass' is created. One possible future is that certain regions on the edge of Europe will go deeper into poverty, because parts of those regions' populations suffer relative poverty within their communities as well as their communities remaining economically excluded within Europe.

Also, as the labour market bifurcates, we shall see pockets of low-paid labour that will attract labour-intensive industry, and other pockets of high-skilled and highly-paid labour that will attract high-technology industry. Development zones might help to bring skills and industry into poor areas, but these compromise the free markets in goods and labour, and thus slow down European social and economic integration.

Part of the answer to social exclusion would be a Citizen's Income. A Europe-wide Citizen's Income would not only assist the free movement of labour, but it would also offer to people a small secure income to cushion the social and economic disturbances that accompany the free movement of goods, services and labour. A Europe-wide Citizen's Income (with the level probably related to the cost of living) would also distribute financial resources from wealthier parts of Europe to the poorer parts, making inefficient adjustment funds less necessary.

Social exclusion will not be solved by a Citizen's Income, but it could help. European nation states should grant to the European Commission and the European Parliament the ability to make it happen.

## 73

# A Citizen's Income could work at different levels

A Citizen's Income would certainly work at the level of the nation state. In federal states it could work at the level below the nation state: for instance, at provincial level in Canada, or at state level in the USA. All that would be required for a subnational Citizen's Income would be a robust list of citizens resident at the subnational level. In such semi-federal nation states as the United Kingdom, existing experience of devolved government suggests that a Citizen's Income could work in each of England, Wales, Scotland, and Northern Ireland. Again, all that would be required would be complete and accurate lists of citizens resident in each of them. Scotland recently made use of such a list to hold its referendum on independence.

Whether a Citizen's Income could be administered at more local levels is an interesting question. Individuals and households move frequently within the countries in which they live, and within the states and provinces of federated states. The UK's new locally regulated means-tested property tax rebate, Council Tax Support, suggests that means-tested benefits can be managed differently in different locations, so we should expect Citizen's Income administrations to be able to keep track of who was living where. But adjusting personal tax allowances only in those localities in which a Citizen's Income was in payment could be too much to ask. Local Citizen's Income schemes are probably not on the agenda for developed economies. Local pilot projects in India and Namibia have shown that it is possible to administer temporary Citizen's Incomes at the local level in developing countries, but those local experiments were plagued by migration into the pilot communities, so permanent local schemes would probably not be viable.

Countries in the European Union already have free markets in labour, goods and services, and countries in other regions of the world are moving in this direction. A Citizen's Income at bloc level would make a lot of sense.

The really interesting question is whether a global Citizen's Income would be possible. Why not? It could be funded by income tax collected within each country, or by regional or global carbon or financial transaction taxes. Such a Citizen's Income could reduce poverty around the world, and therefore reduce both armed conflicts and migration flows. Everyone would benefit. While a global Citizen's Income is some way off, and we must clearly concentrate on implementing Citizen's Incomes at more local levels, there is no reason not to look forward to a time when every individual living on this planet will receive an unconditional, non-withdrawable income.

## 74

# A Citizen's Income of any size would be useful

A Citizen's Income of any size – even a very small one – would have beneficial effects.

It would reduce marginal deduction rates; if a Citizen's Income were to replace just some of somebody's means-tested benefits, then, as earnings rose, means-tested benefits would be withdrawn, but the Citizen's Income would not be. As the individual or household would be on lower amounts of means-tested benefits, as their earnings rose they would more quickly than before reach the point at which means-tested benefits had all been withdrawn, and from that point onwards no further benefits withdrawal would take place. They would therefore find it easier to earn their way out of poverty.

For people not on means-tested benefits, their Citizen's Income would replace all or part of their personal tax allowance. For them, the tax system would operate as before. Their marginal deduction rates would not be affected.

So a small Citizen's Income would have either beneficial effects on households' marginal deduction rates, or no effects at all.

However small the Citizen's Income, some households would find that occasional or part-time earnings would for the first time enable them to leave means-tested benefits behind. Fraud and error rates would be reduced; fewer people would be subject to cohabitation tests, work tests, or sanctions; and administrative costs would fall. The cost of administering the small Citizen's Income would be negligible compared to the saving that would accrue from households leaving means-tested benefits.

A Citizen's Income of any size would go to every citizen and so would improve social cohesion; it would contribute to a sense of shared and individual citizenship; and it would give to numerous households more flexibility over their employment patterns, and more ability to undertake voluntary community work. For students it would provide a base on which to build with loans, grants, and employment; for the pre-retired it would provide the employment flexibility that would enable them to ease their way into retirement; and for carers it would provide a foundation on which to build earnings and other benefits.

It is sometimes suggested that a small Citizen's Income would not be worth the trouble. The administration of a Citizen's Income would be so simple, and the transition so easy, that to establish a small Citizen's Income would be very little trouble. As we have seen, it would certainly be worth it. As we experienced the advantages offered by our Citizen's Income, we would want to see it grow; and the fact that everybody would receive it would result in the necessary political pressure.

## 75

# A Citizen's Income would be both desirable and feasible

There are many policies that would be desirable but not feasible. Free public transport, for everyone, and from anywhere to anywhere, would be such a policy. The policy would be desirable as it would get lots of cars off the roads, but trains and buses would be quickly swamped, new provision would be constantly required, and the public subsidy needed would be unsustainable. Public transport has to be rationed, and the price mechanism is one way of doing that. The practical solution is a balance between individual payment and public subsidy.

And there are plenty of policies that are feasible but not desirable. Reducing tax rates to zero and abolishing all public services would be feasible, but would not be desirable. There are many services that can only be provided efficiently as public services, so public provision, and the taxation to pay for it, is in general desirable. The practical question is where the balance should be struck between individuals providing for themselves and government bodies providing for everyone through tax-funded public services.

The policy that is both feasible and desirable is rare. A Citizen's Income would be such a policy.

A Citizen's Income would be desirable. It would improve social cohesion, would increase equality, would enable people more easily to earn their way out of poverty, and would give people more freedom over their personal relationships and their employment patterns.

A Citizen's Income would also be feasible. It would be administratively feasible, because it would be easy to administer, and because transition to a benefits system based on a Citizen's Income would be possible to manage; it would be financially feasible, because revenue neutral schemes are available, and some of those schemes would impose no losses on low-earning households; and it could be politically feasible, because every mainstream political ideology can find reasons for supporting the idea. Once implemented, a Citizen's Income would be psychologically feasible.

There are some aspects of a Citizen's Income that would serve both its desirability and its feasibility. For instance, the administrative simplicity of a Citizen's Income would contribute to its feasibility, and a Citizen's Income's administrative simplicity would mean that it would be transparent – that is, everyone would know how it worked – which is a desirable characteristic of any social policy and of any benefits system.

The fact that a Citizen's Income is both feasible and desirable is a characteristic to be treasured. It is unfortunate that this unusual combination will not on its own ensure the implementation of a Citizen's Income scheme.

## 76

# A Citizen's Income would be financially feasible

The fundamental question is, of course: 'Can we afford it?' The obvious answer is 'Yes', in the short term. In numerous countries central banks have created new money which they have used to purchase government bonds, enabling governments to rescue the banks. The only reason this money could not be distributed equally to every citizen was that there was no administrative mechanism that could do that.

But unless central banks become the only source of new money, the creation of money by central banks will remain an occasional activity, so in the foreseeable future any Citizen's Income will need to be funded by reducing personal tax allowances and means-tested and other benefits, and possibly by increasing income tax rates slightly. If the value of the Citizen's Income is close to the value of means-tested benefits, and also close to the value of personal tax allowances, then it will always be possible to fund a Citizen's Income in this way. A revenue neutral scheme will therefore always be possible; that is, we shall be able to pay for a Citizen's Income without seeking additional funding from outside the tax and benefits systems. Revenue neutrality is the most important criterion for a Citizen's Income's financial feasibility, and it is a criterion that we can meet.

But there is another sense in which a Citizen's Income would need to be financially feasible. Because of the complexities of most tax and benefits systems, a Citizen's Income funded by adjustments to the existing tax and benefits systems will result in gains for some households and losses for others. Take just one UK example of the problem. Means-tested benefits pay less to a couple than they would have paid in total to the two individuals if they had been living apart. A Citizen's Income would be paid at the same rate to every individual, so, at the transition, individuals would suffer losses, and couples would experience gains. A further two criteria will therefore be required. To be financially feasible, a Citizen's Income scheme will need to impose no losses on low-income households, and it will need to impose no substantial losses on other households.

Research has shown that it is perfectly possible to fulfil all three of our criteria in the UK context,[8] and given that the UK's benefits system is as complex as any, we can assume that the same set of conditions can be fulfilled elsewhere too.

## 77

# A Citizen's Income would be administratively feasible

Of all of the feasibility tests that a Citizen's Income would need to pass – tests for administrative, institutional, psychological, political, behavioural, and financial feasibility – by far the easiest test for it to pass would be that for administrative feasibility.

The 'administrative feasibility' question is in fact two questions: 1) Would it be possible to administer a Citizen's Income? And 2) Would it be possible to administer the transition to a system based on a Citizen's Income?

There are already countries with universal unconditional benefits. New Zealand, Denmark and the Netherlands have Citizen's Pensions; [9] the UK has a universal Child Benefit, and a Winter Fuel Allowance paid at the same rate to everyone over state pension age; and the UK also has a National Health Service that is universal, is free at the point of use for every legal resident, and is ranked by the Washington-based Commonwealth Fund as the second cheapest and the most efficient of the eleven OECD health care systems that it studied (the United States' own system came last). [10] We know how to manage universal and unconditional welfare systems, and a Citizen's Income would be no more difficult to administer than the UK's Child Benefit. All that it would require would be a list of citizens and their bank account details, and for those few individuals without a bank account it would be easy to organise payment through a local post office.

As for administration of the transition to a Citizen's Income, much would depend on the implementation method chosen. Either a Citizen's Income could be introduced for everybody, all at the same time, or different age groups could be transferred one after the other, perhaps starting with children (in the UK, only minor amendments to the UK's Child Benefit would be needed), then individuals past state retirement age (the UK's new Single Tier State Pension would be easy to adapt), then young adults and the pre-retired, and finally the age group in the middle. At each stage of a Citizen's Income's implementation, personal tax allowances would be reduced and means-tested and other benefits would be either recalculated for each claimant or abolished altogether, depending on the implementation method chosen. None of this would be difficult – and in the UK it would be much easier than the current transition from multiple means-tested benefits to the single new and misnamed means-tested benefit 'Universal Credit'.

# 78

## A Citizen's Income would be institutionally feasible

The question is this: given what we know about the ways in which social policies travel through the policy process, from idea to implementation, can we envisage ways in which a Citizen's Income would be able to negotiate that journey? ('Institutional feasibility' is about the institutions of the policy-making process. Other writers call it 'policy process feasibility' or 'strategic feasibility'.)

Policy ideas reside in all kinds of places: books, the internet, think tanks, political parties, university departments, and government departments, to name but a few. To be implemented, ideas need to be able to travel through a complex institutional network, and particularly along the routes through think tanks, political parties, government departments, governments, and parliaments. Think tanks are particularly interesting as they enable political parties to hold internal debates without laying themselves open to accusations of disunity. The journey will be influenced by public opinion and by such self-interested players as computer companies; and certain policy characteristics might facilitate the journey, for instance, continuity with existing policy, and coherence with stated government priorities. Feasibility tests will usually need to be passed – but not always very thoroughly if a government wishes to implement a policy for political reasons. Electoral advantage will always be a factor.

Sometimes a government or a think tank will carry out a pilot project. We have seen Citizen's Income pilot projects in Namibia and India, but no true Citizen's Income pilot in a developed economy. (Negative Income Tax experiments in Canada and the USA have provided us with useful information, but they were not Citizen's Income pilot projects.)

There is plenty of written material on Citizen's Income schemes, and a global network of informed individuals is in place. Given the number of reasons for taking the Citizen's Income idea seriously, detailed consideration by think tanks and government departments is not difficult to imagine. This could generate further media attention, and we can envisage sufficient numbers of ministers, shadow ministers, and members of parliament, in a variety of political parties, being persuaded that means-testing and other complexities have had their day and that an extension of universal benefits should be given a try. Public education would lead to sufficient public understanding, and this would provide the conditions for ministerial commitment and then legislation.

So we can see how a Citizen's Income could successfully negotiate the policy process. A Citizen's Income is institutionally feasible. Whether a Citizen's Income scheme will succeed in making the journey from idea to implementation is of course another matter.

# 79

## A Citizen's Income would be behaviourally feasible

Before a Citizen's Income could be implemented, it would need to show that it was administratively, financially, and politically feasible, and that it could pilot its way through the policy process ('institutional feasibility'). A Citizen's Income would also need to be psychologically feasible: that is, people would need to understand the idea and want it to happen. But behavioural feasibility is different. A policy is behaviourally feasible if it improves people's situations in practice, and this can only be tested after implementation.

We can make an informed guess that a Citizen's Income would prove to be behaviourally feasible because it would provide a financial floor on which individuals and households could build a diverse structure of incomes, and it would give to people a greater degree of choice in the employment market. We can reasonably expect that the greater ability to increase disposable income as earned income rises would be much valued once it was experienced; that people would marvel at the simplicity of the administration of their Citizen's Income; and that those who had experienced work tests or cohabitation tests would value the absence of them. Those families able to come off means-tested benefits would be glad to see the back of calculation errors, overpayments, and demands for repayment. Some people would no doubt enjoy the fact that everybody received a Citizen's Income, from the poorest person in the country to the wealthiest; and everyone would experience an enhanced sense of individual and shared citizenship.

We can also expect that businesses would value the greater employment market flexibility that a Citizen's Income would offer to them, that benefits administrators would not be sorry to see the back of work tests, sanctions, and cohabitation tests, and that local authorities would be very willing to match local people to local employment, and to provide appropriate skills training, as some already do. We can expect that the courts would be pleased to see a significant reduction in benefits fraud. Only civil servants might be sorry to see a reduction of people dependent on means-tested benefits, but they too would receive Citizen's Incomes and would find themselves with new employment options.

But however much we can reasonably suppose that a Citizen's Income would pass a behavioural feasibility test, it remains true that the test can only be passed after implementation, and that until implementation occurs many people will remain doubtful. Informed cross-party consensus and leadership will therefore be essential.

80

# A Citizen's Income could be psychologically feasible

Many of the groups of people to whom I speak are already persuaded that a Citizen's Income is a good idea; but I also speak to groups in which most of the members haven't heard of a Citizen's Income, or are sceptical, or are opposed. Here the task is more interesting.

I might define a Citizen's Income and offer some of the reasons outlined in this book in relation to marginal withdrawal rates, employment patterns, and household structure; I might compare a Citizen's Income with Child Benefit; and I might try a thought experiment, and ask the group how they would design tax and benefits systems for a community without either of them. As I look around the room, I can see the penny dropping for some members of the group, sometimes rapidly, sometimes slowly; but for other members of the group, the penny never drops.

For some people, the existing categories in their minds are so embedded that every new idea has to be fitted into one of them: so they might try to fit a Citizen's Income into the 'National Minimum Wage' category, or the means-tested benefits category, or the contributory benefits category – and of course, it doesn't fit, so it is parked in the 'too difficult' box. Other members might understand the concept of a Citizen's Income perfectly well, but be unable to get past such common objections as 'the rich don't need it' or 'people will stop working'. For some, such terms as 'targeting' are so significant that they cannot believe that as earnings rose we would choose not to extract some of the benefits that the State was paying to them. Whatever the blockage – the penny hasn't dropped.

But perhaps more important than the fact that for some people the penny doesn't drop is the fact that for some people it does. Following the logic, or understanding the parallels with other universal and unconditional benefits, has enabled them to think differently, to see that means-testing isn't inevitable, and that, in the context of a progressive income tax system, an unconditional and non-withdrawable benefit is really rather sensible.

This reason is titled 'A Citizen's Income *could* be psychologically feasible', not '… would be…'. A social policy is psychologically feasible when a sufficient number of people understand it and the reason for trying it. It is perfectly possible for people to understand a Citizen's Income, and to appreciate both its desirability and its feasibility. The only question is how many people will, and how many will not.

## 81

# A Citizen's Income could be attractive to centre-right parties

One of the Citizen's Income proposal's most consistent advocates in the UK's House of Commons during the 1980s was the late Sir Brandon Rhys Williams, a Conservative Member of Parliament. An important reason for his support was that a Citizen's Income would make it possible for people to take whatever employment was on offer and to benefit financially from it. [11] It has generally been Conservative politicians who have understood the damage that high marginal deduction rates do to employment incentives. During the 1980s it was a Conservative Secretary of State, Norman Fowler, whose reforms of means-tested benefits were designed to reduce the amounts of benefits that people lost as their earnings rose; and the current Secretary of State Iain Duncan Smith's amalgamation of several benefits into one means-tested benefit, Universal Credit, with a lower total withdrawal rate, has the same end in view. Every individual should be able to react in the same way to economic incentives, so everyone should be able to benefit from increased earnings, and low earners should not experience marginal deduction rates higher than those experienced by the wealthy.

Centre-right arguments can sometimes be stated in terms of what a Citizen's Income would not do. A Citizen's Income would not create dependency; and it would not discourage people from taking employment. More positively, for a healthy economy industry needs to be efficient, which requires a market in labour that is as free as possible from rigidities. The current benefits system imposes numerous rigidities on the employment market, whereas a Citizen's Income would not.

For the centre-right, social solidarity, individual liberty, and individual responsibility belong together. There is no suggestion here of income equality, but rather that a Citizen's Income would enable the widespread educational opportunity that would develop potential and would thus enrich all of us. There is no suggestion here of increasing taxation in order to pay for more public services, but rather that we ought to order our life together so that people are more able to take responsibility for their own economic situation. A Citizen's Income would encourage employment, self-employment, education and training, would remove bureaucrats from people's lives, and would provide individuals with more freedom of choice. There is not a lot for a centre-right politician not to like about a Citizen's Income, and much of which to approve.

## 82

# A Citizen's Income has attractions for trades unions

It is understandable that trades unions have concentrated their attention on active participants in the labour force and not on those who might wish to be in it but are not: hence longstanding interest in income tax rates and allowances (which benefit employees), contributory benefits (which benefit employees), occupational pensions (which benefit employees), and a National Minimum Wage (which benefits employees), and less so in universal benefits, or the earnings rules attached to means-tested benefits.

The same history might be the reason for lack of interest in a Citizen's Income. An additional reason for this neglect might be trade union officers' understanding that a Citizen's Income would provide a secure income floor, and so might reduce trades unions' control over their members' subsistence incomes. A Citizen's Income would also herald an even more flexible labour market, the consequences of which for trade union membership levels would be difficult to predict.

Trades Unions often call for 'proper jobs', by which they mean work that is paid, secure, and with good conditions; and in a situation in which only paid employment can provide self-worth and an adequate income, and in which benefits regulations stop people from climbing out of poverty, we need as much high wage work as possible. But it does not need to be like this, and a Citizen's Income would help it to change. It could be in trades unions' interests to advocate a Citizen's Income if this gave people more choice to refuse lousy jobs.

A Citizen's Income would turn the employment market into something closer to a true market in labour, in which people would be in a better position to decline unpleasant work: so in many occupations conditions and wages would improve; a Citizen's Income would make part-time employment and self-employment more attractive, and would make it more worthwhile for people to accept low-paying jobs, and could therefore increase trade union membership; with increased memberships, trades unions would be better able to negotiate over wage rates; and in a flourishing economy, trades unions would be needed for coordinated action over safety at work and employment law.

As automation continues, trades unions will increasingly see the virtues of a Citizen's Income; and if support among political parties were to turn into a real chance of a Citizen's Income being implemented, then the trades unions could be among those organisations seeking such a reform. Trades unions need have no fundamental objections or significant anxieties in relation to a Citizen's Income, and we might even find trades unions leading the campaign for implementation.

## 83

# A Citizen's Income could be attractive to centre-left parties

An interesting fact about the Citizen's Income movement around the world is that individuals from right across the political spectrum are involved in it, from neoliberals, through centre-right parties, centre parties, and centre-left parties, and then on to genuine socialists.

Interest among socialists in particular is no surprise. Socialism is about equality, and the abolition of poverty, and to both of these a Citizen's Income would contribute; and for those socialists attracted to Marx's complaints about employees being alienated from the product of their labour, a Citizen's Income should be attractive because it would encourage small businesses, cooperatives, and self-employment. Socialism is a broad church that includes Marxists, communists, trades unionists who want to extract from capitalist industry the highest possible returns for employees, 'clause 4 socialists' committed to the nationalisation of industry, and socialists committed to equality of outcome as well as equality of opportunity. Socialists of all kinds can support a Citizen's Income because it could create to the kind of society that they want to build.

Further along the spectrum are the centre-left parties that sometimes find themselves in government. They believe that capitalist firms and their regulation can often reap more public benefit than nationalisation, that an employee deserves a just wage and good working conditions, that private property is legitimate, that equality of opportunity is an essential route to greater equality of outcomes, and that enterprise, democracy, and pluralism are essential to a modern society.

For a centre-left party, a Citizen's Income would offer a fundamental equality that would cohere with a continuing socialist ideology; it would facilitate greater equality of opportunity, particularly for young adults in training and education; and it would enable the employment market to behave more like a market, which would offer wages that more nearly reflected the value of someone's work, and that would offer better working conditions because it would be easier for people to decline bad jobs. A Citizen's Income would offer an enhanced sense of shared citizenship; and because revenue neutral schemes are possible, a Citizen's Income would not require additional public funding, and so could not be accused of being unaffordable. A Citizen's Income would cohere with both the socialist and the trade union roots of most centre-left parties, and it would serve those parties well as they adapt to a fast-changing world. It is high time that centre-left parties took a hard look at a Citizen's Income.

84

# A Citizen's Income would be attractive to centre parties

Political debate is frequently less than enlightening, and often descends into complaining about what the other parties have done or are doing. During election campaigns, the argument is all about which leader you might trust to govern the country; and then, and at other times, it is the media that define the terms of any policy debate rather than the parties themselves. Rarely do parties have the opportunity to discuss their political ideologies, and to explain the consequences of those ideologies for social policy.

The UK's Liberal Democratic Party was formed in 1988 when the short-lived Social Democrats (which split from the Labour Party) joined the longstanding Liberal Party (committed to personal freedom). Now the Liberal Democrats locate themselves in the 'radical centre'. During the 1990s the party committed itself to a Citizen's Income because it was committed to a 'citizenship society', a society in which individuals would have the opportunity to better themselves and their communities, and to take responsibility for their lives and for the life of society. Paddy Ashdown, the leader at the time, and many members of the party, were convinced that a Citizen's Income would be the best way to move on from the Beveridge Report in a way appropriate to new times. (Beveridge himself had been a member of the Liberal Party.) But then the Liberal Democrats abandoned the policy, not because they thought that there was anything wrong with it, but because members believed that they would find it difficult to sell it to the electorate.

Since 2010 the Liberal Democrats have been in a coalition government with the Conservative Party: a liaison from which they are now trying to extract themselves in preparation for a General Election.

A small third party that is sandwiched between two larger parties on either side of it on the political spectrum will always find it difficult to define what it stands for, for it is bound to look as if every policy is a compromise between those of the other parties, and that all that the third party can do is criticise the larger parties. The UK Liberal Democrats' espousal of a Citizen's Income was a brief exercise in genuine distinctiveness, and one that the party might usefully repeat. Similar 'sandwiched' parties elsewhere might also wish to consider a Citizen's Income as a distinctive contribution to political debate.

A Citizen's Income is not a compromise, and it is not a negative swipe at other parties. It is quite simply a good idea.

# 85

# A Citizen's Income is attractive to people who care about the environment

The UK's Green Party has shown considerable interest in a Citizen's Income. This interest is not without its critics, for some suggest that a Citizen's Income might make the economy more efficient and thus lead to natural resources being used up faster. However, commitment to a Citizen's Income by the Green Party in the UK is carefully thought out. One important argument is that it is difficult to ask people to take thought for the planet if they do not have sufficient income to enable them to participate effectively in community activity. Another is that a Citizen's Income would give people far more choices, and that many of those choices would be good for the environment. Craft industries, small-scale organic agriculture, and solar and wind power generation are often local initiatives involving small groups of people working together. Such activities would reduce the need for the products of the kinds of industry that destroy the environment, and they would be easier to undertake if every citizen had a small income on which they could rely.

James Robertson suggests that we could be destined for an automated society, in which a few people are technically competent and wealthy, and in which the rest become an underclass (even if no one is starving); or we could be destined for a diverse society in which people choose their own kinds of work, paid and unpaid, and in which technology and automation offer widespread benefits to the whole of society in terms of both welfare and responsibility. He believes that a Citizen's Income could help to launch the latter kind of society. But the role that a Citizen's Income could play might in fact be more important than Robertson imagines. A Citizen's Income might be a necessary condition for ensuring that we go down the latter road rather than the former; and it is not impossible that it could be a sufficient condition, too.

In the UK, the Green Party has committed itself to establishing a Citizen's Income: but it is not just members of Green parties who want zero carbon dioxide emissions, to conserve the natural environment, and preserve species diversity. Anyone committed to a society in harmony with a sustainable environment should ask themselves whether a Citizen's Income would be more likely to serve such a society. In the short term, funding a Citizen's Income by adjusting the tax and benefits systems would deliver the environmental benefits that we have discussed. In the longer term, a Citizen's Income funded by a carbon tax would offer both those environmental benefits and more besides.

# 86

# A Citizen's Income would be politically feasible

A Citizen's Income is administratively feasible because of its simplicity, and we could manage the transition; it is potentially psychologically feasible, because conversion from commitment to means-testing to seeing the advantages of universal benefits is perfectly possible; it is institutionally feasible because we can envisage routes through the policy process; and it could be behaviourally feasible as it would improve individuals' and households' financial positions and give them more control over their lives. But would a Citizen's Income be politically feasible? It would be, because it can fit easily within both the ideology and the immediate interests of any mainstream political party. Admittedly there would be no immediate votes in a Citizen's Income, but because the policy can be argued for, and because existing universal benefits provide us with precedents, education and consultation followed by legislation could meet with public approval. There will always be members of parliament who believe that means-testing helps the poor: but they, like members of the public, are rational people, and are therefore perfectly capable of understanding the advantages of universal benefits and the disadvantages of means-testing once these are explained.

It is never easy to define in a few short sentences what different political parties stand for, because each party is a broad coalition of interests, and each of them reacts to the political currents of their time. But, in broad outline, whether a party stands for an enterprise culture, for public provision, for equality of opportunity, for equality of outcome, for the freedom of the individual, or for a cohesive society, its members can understand the ways in which a Citizen's Income would give more people an element of equality, the opportunity to increase their income, and more choices as to what to do with their lives, and to society greater social justice and improved social cohesion.

The differences between parties often mask basic agreements between them. Members of all parties want to see people taking initiative, fulfilling their potential, and creating sustainable communities. The different broad outlines that I have offered are thus more to do with emphasis, and with the means of obtaining a variety of ends, than with the ends themselves. This means that cross-party agreement to implement a Citizen's Income would not be difficult to achieve.

A Citizen's Income would be politically feasible. Add the different feasibilities together and we can see that a Citizen's Income would be simply feasible.

# E
# IDEAS

# 87

## A Citizen's Income would promote liberty

'Liberty' is a difficult concept because, like many abstract notions, we have to give the word some definition if it is not to be meaningless, and one person's definition will not be another's. Definition sometimes has to be negative: that is, we know where there is not liberty, even if we are not quite sure where there is; and definition sometimes has to be relative: that is, given two situations, we can sometimes agree that someone would have more liberty in one situation than they would have in another. But positive definition remains a problem.

Liberty is a particularly difficult concept to define because one person's liberty can constrain another's. My liberty to do as I wish in my family, in a company, or on the currency markets can diminish other people's liberty. An investment banker's liberty to close down a factory in order to increase a company's profits constrains the liberty of the people who worked in that factory and who might now not be able to choose where to go on holiday, or whether to go on holiday at all.

A similar problem arises when we try to legislate for liberty. Lower taxes might give greater economic liberty to some while reducing the educational and healthcare opportunities of others, thus reducing their liberty, whereas to raise tax rates might constrain the spending decisions of the well-off while increasing other people's educational opportunities. Rarely can social policy increase some people's liberty while not reducing others'.

A Citizen's Income is interesting because it would increase a lot of people's liberty and would not need to reduce significantly anybody else's. If somebody's means-tested benefits were turned into universal benefits, then at the point of implementation they would not experience the additional liberty that increased disposable income would offer, but they would find themselves with more employment pattern options, more options for increasing their disposable income, more choices over their use of time, and greater freedom from bureaucratic interference. If income tax rates needed to rise slightly in order to fund a Citizen's Income, then some people's economic liberty might be slightly constrained, but such constraint would be minimal compared to the increased liberty experienced by households and individuals who suddenly found themselves freed from means-tested benefits.

There are many constraints on liberty that a Citizen's Income would not alter, but if a Citizen's Income will increase some people's liberty substantially while not decreasing significantly that of anybody else, then it is a rare kind of social policy, and we ought to give it a try.

## 88

# A Citizen's Income would offer greater equality

'Those who dread a dead-level of income and wealth, which is not at the moment, perhaps, a very pressing danger in England, do not dread, it seems, a dead-level of law and order, and of security for life and property.'[1]

Whether or not we think that the essential tasks would still be done if everyone received exactly the same income, R.H. Tawney has a point. A healthy society requires a basic equality of opportunity, and an adequate income is essential to that. For income and wealth to be concentrated in fewer and fewer hands, and for fewer and fewer people to be able to increase their income and wealth, is to depress the overall level of opportunity in society, and is thus to depress economic activity. Inequality is bad for everybody.

There is a variety of measures of inequality. A more recent one is the Palma: the ratio of the top 10% of the population's share of gross national income (GNI) to the share of the poorest 40%.[2] A recent OECD report recognises the importance of this measure: 'The biggest factor for the impact of inequality on growth is the gap between lower income households and the rest of the population.'[3] Selective benefits exacerbate the problem, whereas universal benefits reduce inequality by benefiting people in the lowest four earnings deciles along with everyone else.[4]

Throughout our lives we all receive both public and private resources, and we generate both public and private wealth. It would therefore be entirely right for the basic requirement for life in a civilized society – an income – to be provided both by a free and equal social gift and by individual hard work. There is no contradiction here. A Citizen's Income would both increase equality and encourage the kind of creativity that can offer highly unequal financial rewards.

If we are serious about both reducing inequality and encouraging enterprise, then there could be no better place to start than by implementing a Citizen's Income.

# 89

# A Citizen's Income would generate social solidarity

'Fraternity', being a male-oriented word, is now perhaps better expressed by the term 'social solidarity'. This would make 'liberty, equality and social solidarity' the motto that the French Revolution bequeathed to France. Social solidarity is perhaps even more difficult to define than equality and liberty. We can tell when it has broken down, but that does not mean that we know what it is, or how to make it happen. Negatively, it is an absence of social fractures: of the social gulfs – between people's contexts, values, cultures and outlooks – that make it difficult to maintain a well-functioning society in which everyone can flourish. Social solidarity is not a dissolution of the differences between our cultures, values and outlooks; rather, it is a depth of understanding between people in different positions in society – an understanding underpinned by sufficient levels of shared experience and institutions. Take healthcare as an example. The United States has a wide variety of schemes: means-tested systems for the elderly and for the general population; privately run and government regulated insurance schemes for the working age population (recently extended to larger numbers of people under President Obama's scheme); and private insurance for anyone who can afford it. US society is fractured in terms of healthcare, so its healthcare system does not promote social solidarity, and it is itself a symptom of a lack of social solidarity. The UK, on the other hand, experiences a significant social solidarity in relation to healthcare. The National Health Service is free at the point of use for any legal resident. Those who can afford to will sometimes buy insurance or pay for healthcare so that they can jump the queue, but the healthcare will generally be of the same quality. The NHS is both source and result of significant social solidarity.

If this is what we mean by social solidarity, then a Citizen's Income would increase it, for it would include all of us in a shared experience of receiving an unconditional and non-withdrawable income.

Whenever the terms 'fraternity' or 'social solidarity' are used (just as when 'liberty' and 'equality' are used) we must ask what definition the user is giving to it. With careful and not too ambitious usage, the words 'liberty', 'equality' and 'fraternity' or 'social solidarity' can still be useful as we shape social policy. All three of them demand a Citizen's Income as one of the pillars of a free society in which everyone can experience their fundamental human equality and their mutual belonging.

## 90

# A Citizen's Income would enhance social justice

'Justice' is one of those words that we all use but that we all find difficult to define. Without the word, we would find moral judgment about the direction of our society impossible, but as with 'equality', 'liberty' and 'fraternity', we find positive definition difficult. However, as with those other ideals, we can sometimes agree that one situation is more just than another, and perhaps that is sufficient. In the UK, it is surely unjust that someone on means-tested benefits might see only a £15 increase in their disposable income if they earn an extra £100, whereas someone earning large amounts of money might see their disposable income increase by £53 if they earn an extra £100. This is a clear injustice, and one that a Citizen's Income would go a long way to repairing.

A just society is one in which its members experience justice. We might all have access to the law, the right to vote, and the right to stand for election, but if we suffer from economic injustice then we do not live in a just society. As with situations facing individuals, we can often judge one society to be more just than another, and we can discuss the economic policies that might create a more just society. Economic justice requires that most people should be able to improve their financial position through the exercise of ability, initiative, and hard work. Because a Citizen's Income would tackle the poverty and unemployment traps, it would increase economic justice for large numbers of people. Thus a Citizen's Income would create a more just society.

For Plato, a just city is one in which the citizens harmoniously fulfil their distinctive roles, in the same way as a just person is one in whose soul the appetitive, spirited and rational elements all function harmoniously. We might object to the enforced stratification of the society that Plato recommended in *The Republic*, but his basic instinct is correct: that a just society will be one in which everyone can undertake their own projects and fulfil their own potential at the same time as living in harmony with everyone else who is doing that. In today's world the rigidities of most modern tax and benefits systems make that difficult to achieve. The flexibility that a Citizen's Income would grant to the employment market, and to each individual's employment pattern, would make it much more likely to happen. A Citizen's Income could, perhaps surprisingly, deliver Plato's just society, without requiring the kind of role enforcement that Plato envisaged.

# 91

## A Citizen's Income would be fair

'Fairness' is similar to 'justice', 'liberty', and 'equality'. We cannot define 'justice' in any absolute sense, and the idea that there is such a thing as justice apart from particular manifestations of it is an ancient Greek prejudice. Similarly with 'fairness'. We use 'fairness' differently in different situations, without either the possibility or the necessity of discovering some core definition that is universally applicable (although there will be 'family resemblances' [5] between the different uses of the word). And as with justice and liberty, we can identify situations that are fairer than others, and societies that are fairer than others, without closely defining fairness itself.

John Rawls has given to 'justice' a definition that I would rather offer as a partial definition of 'fairness', for it would result in what we could all agree to call a 'fairer society'. Rawls' definition is that 'a fair society is one which is acceptable to someone who does not know where he or she personally stands in relation to allocation'. [6] A fair society is one that we could accept if we did not know whether we were going to be a cleaner or a merchant banker, unemployed or employed, and so on. We do have particular positions within our society, so we cannot ever undertake this exercise in practice: but we can work out the kind of society that would fit the definition, and it is likely to be one in which the same rules would apply to everyone.

We do not have such a society at the moment. Some families and individuals are subject to earnings rules, work tests, sanctions, and a cohabitation rule, and some are not. Some households suffer significantly higher withdrawal rates as earnings rise than other households do. Because a Citizen's Income would decrease the number of people on means-tested benefits, and thus the number of people subject to such rules; because a Citizen's Income would begin to equalise the withdrawal rates that different households suffer; and because every citizen would receive a Citizen's Income on the same basis, a Citizen's Income would give to us a society that we could all agree to be fairer than the society in which we now live. There would still be much about such a society that was unfair – and in particular the massive differences in wealth and earned incomes that people experience – but a Citizen's Income would be taking us in the right direction.

# 92

## A Citizen's Income would enhance democracy

There are many countries still without a universal franchise – the most glaring example is of course China – but perhaps they are simply lagging behind. Until a thousand years ago, the only person in any country with any power was the king, and he distributed power to others as he saw fit – until someone challenged him and became king in his place. But then, because the British king needed money from his barons, he had to share power with them, and so the process towards a universal franchise began; and it is thus right that we should regard Britain's Magna Carta as a foundational document for democracy even though its writers would never have believed a universal franchise to be either possible or desirable.

From the gathering of powerful landowners that gave birth to the Magna Carta emerged a parliament and finally elections. Originally elections were restricted to wealthy men, then to more men, and then to women and the whole adult population. At each transition there were arguments on both sides: on the one side the demands of justice and equality; on the other the contention that only certain people understood how to govern and that therefore only they should choose who should govern. The latter argument was at each transition shown to be the prejudice and the self-fulfilling prophecy that it was, for if a society treats a group of people as inferior and incompetent then they will become incompetent and they will feel inferior (and hence most revolutions have been run by intellectuals). The universal franchise, by declaring all of us capable of making decisions, has enabled us to do so.

A Citizen's Income would have a similar effect in the economic sphere to the universal franchise in the political: it would be a statement of citizenship, of membership, and of responsibility, and it would help to create the responsible citizenship society of which the Citizen's Income would be both a symbol and a means. We would one day take it for granted, as we do the universal franchise.

An interesting proposition is that we should connect the Citizen's Income proposal and the universal franchise by employing the electoral register to administer Citizen's Incomes. It would suddenly be in everyone's interests to ensure that the register remained up to date, which it is not now; and a consequence would be that every Citizen's Income recipient would receive at every election a voting card telling them when and where to vote. Democracy would be enhanced.

## 93

# A Citizen's Income would serve the common good

Bill Jordan, social worker and academic, has written a good deal about 'the common good'[7] as the definition of the good society. He makes the point that people in poverty are not primarily looking for a 'sharing out' of resources by those in power, but for a 'sharing in', an opportunity to participate in the life of their community, a community in which people share their lives with one another at the same time as maintaining differing moral codes and belief systems.

Many projects result from individuals choosing to work together, but some transcend the contractual relationship between one individual and another and create such public goods as peace, or a sustainable environment, or a quality of life experienced by a community. Sharing, cooperation and democracy, often coordinated by local or national government, are as important to such cooperative projects as are contracts made in a market-place, so such collaborative activity must be given the weight often reserved for the market alone.

In purely practical terms, the projects that have improved our lives over the past two hundred years have been collaborative public ones: drainage and water systems, mass education, immunisation campaigns, and so on. No amount of individual responsibility could have achieved these. They were collaborative efforts, created by people working together to promote the common good.

Jordan advocates a Citizen's Income because it would enable everyone to 'share in' an equal foundational distribution of wealth (which we cannot do today); it would invite participation in wealth-creating activity; and it would give to people more control over their own lives, and thus a greater ability to take part in community activity. A Citizen's Income would therefore provide the material and psychological foundations for the creation of the common good.

The common good is the sum of those public goods that are created by sharing, cooperation, and democracy, rather than by the making of contracts in the market-place, and such a society can be sustainable as well as just. It is possible to imagine a free society or an equal society that is not sustainable, and easy enough to imagine a non-sustainable free-market society; but what a Citizen's Income offers is the basis for a society in which the common good is created and sustained. For any society that cares about its future, a Citizen's Income is therefore desirable.

## 94

# A Citizen's Income would redefine poverty

Who is better off: the person who earns £15,000 per annum and keeps 15p out of every £1 pay rise, or the one who earns £14,000 per annum and keeps 53p out of every £1 pay rise? Initially the former, but in the longer term the latter.

'Poverty' is not easy to define. One child might have parents who both work full time, have plenty of money, but have little time to spend with their children; another might have parents who both work part time, have less money, and have more time to spend with their children. Which child is poor?

Perhaps we should break down 'poverty' into a variety of different 'poverties': attention poverty, income poverty, housing poverty, environmental poverty, fuel poverty, and so on. But even this does not sufficiently capture the complex reality. As Ruth Lister suggests, 'social exclusion' better reflects the social processes that lead families both into and out of poverty; [8] and as John Hills has shown, there are very few people permanently in poverty (some elderly people are). Individuals and families move in and out of various kinds of poverty, often from one week to the next as wages gyrate, and all of us are supported through changes in our fortunes by a welfare state that cushions the worst falls in fortune – except when it fails to deliver. [9] Poverty is not a static state: it is diverse, and it is a process.

So the question is not only: How can we prevent poverty? But: How can we also help people to climb out of poverty when they are in it?

In relation to income poverty, rigid in-work and out-of-work benefits – whether of the contributory or means-tested varieties – might not be the best method. Systems containing any complexity at all, and particularly those that require decision making to take place when a family's circumstances change, are going to have difficulty keeping up with rapid change. The situation demands a radical simplicity that helps to prevent falls into income poverty and also enables families to climb back out again. A Citizen's Income would provide an unchanging income foundation that would help to prevent slides into poverty, and the low marginal deduction rates would help families to recover from poverty.

# 95

## A Citizen's Income would be universal

Immanuel Kant's eighteenth-century suggestion that a 'categorical imperative' is an obligation that is in principle universalisable (that is, it could apply to everyone everywhere) [10] casts interesting light on any discussion of a Citizen's Income. A Citizen's Income would be universal within the territory in which it was implemented, and so would in principle be universalisable. This would make it a kind of moral imperative.

Two hundred years ago, who would have thought that the world's economy would now be dominated by a handful of transnational corporations, and that vast quantities of information would be transmitted along narrow fibres by beams of light? The pace of change will not slacken. Information and communication technology will continue to develop, and markets in goods and services will continue to globalise. Whether this is a good thing or not is another matter (and developing countries in particular might be better off both culturally and economically with a few trade barriers in place), but global markets in goods, services, and eventually in labour, will probably happen – and yet little has been done to create a benefits structure that will take into account these colossal changes. In economies in which innovation and automation are the norms, social security must behave likewise, for it is as much a part of the economy as is any other financial institution.

With a Europe-wide market in goods and labour, it could be useful to establish a Europe-wide social security system, particular as different countries' economies converge; and with markets globalising, it could be useful to establish a global benefits system to reduce poverty traps and prevent poverty globally. A Europe-wide Citizen's Income, and then a global one, would offer integration, and at the same time a platform for national experiment.

We have seen pilot projects in India and Namibia, and we have seen something like a Citizen's Income established by accident in Iran, [11] but we still await a true national Citizen's Income. We shall no doubt wait longer for a European Citizen's Income, and longer still for a global one; but what is important here is that a Citizen's Income is in principle universalisable, and that that is a good reason for starting the process.

# 96

## A Citizen's Income would be beautiful

Can a social security system be beautiful? I do not see why not. The UK's current system is, quite simply, ugly: a diagram to describe the workings of the system is horrendously complicated, with lines and boxes all over the place. Diagrams of other countries' systems are similarly less than beautiful. The diagram of a Citizen's Income, on the other hand, is simple – and any complexities will be more to do with the tax system, or with the bits of contributory and means-tested systems that would be left running, than with the Citizen's Income itself. Whether you call the Citizen's Income diagram beautiful is a matter of opinion, but it certainly has simplicity, and I would say a sparse beauty. If morality and a sparse beauty have anything to do with each other, then a Citizen's Income is going to appeal.

A Citizen's Income will appeal in another sense, too. Tax and benefits systems tend to become more complicated over time as new circumstances require changes to be made, and one change leads to another, and then anomalies need to be sorted out, so yet more changes are made. A Citizen's Income would remain as it is – unless, of course, it ceased to be a Citizen's Income and became something else. A Citizen's Income would retain its simplicity and its beauty, as the UK's Child Benefit has done.

A Citizen's Income's sparse beauty would offer some worthwhile consequences, of course: efficiency, transparency, and predictability. An intriguing possibility is that there could be interesting longer term consequences elsewhere in the system, for to run an attractively simple social security system would be to take such attributes seriously where few people would expect anybody to do so, and this might inspire us to seek beauty elsewhere in our life together: perhaps in healthcare and in education. A particularly interesting challenge would be to create a more elegant tax system. After all, now that computers have replaced the tax tables that employers and tax offices used to use to work out individuals' tax liabilities, there is no reason why higher income tax rates should not be described algebraically by a smooth parabola.

For anyone who seeks beauty in every part of the structure of society, a Citizen's Income is going to be attractive, and might return us to Plato's connections between beauty, justice, and the good. But I recognise that there are still a few who prefer ornate baroque, and for them a means-tested benefits system might remain preferable.

## 97

# A Citizen's Income has a long history

The idea can be traced as far back as Thomas Paine at the end of the eighteenth century. The land belongs to all of us, but it has been expropriated by a few. The few therefore owe to every citizen some compensation. Hence the argument for a Citizen's Income.

In Britain during the 1930s, James Meade advocated a 'Social Dividend', payable to all citizens; [12] and in 1943 Juliet Rhys Williams advocated a non-withdrawable income for each individual as an alternative to the Beveridge Report's prescription of contributory and means-tested benefits. Rhys Williams' idea was not quite that of a Citizen's Income because entitlement would have depended on a work test, but it came very close. Meade later developed Rhys Williams' ideas, abandoning her work test, and financing the scheme through Income Tax.

In Holland the Dutch were discussing 'Basisinkommen' by the late 1970s; in Britain, the first official use of the term 'Basic Income' was in 1982, when Sir Brandon Rhys Williams MP (son of Juliet Rhys Williams) submitted a Citizen's Income scheme in evidence to the House of Commons Treasury and Civil Service Select Committee subcommittee on income distribution; and in 1972, Edward Heath's government put forward detailed proposals for a tax credit scheme, which would have replaced most income tax allowances and some social security benefits with tax credits payable in cash where they exceeded tax liability. These tax credits closely resembled a Citizen's Income, but did not cover the whole population. In 1974, the Heath government fell, and in 1979 Child Benefit (which closely resembles a Citizen's Income for children) was introduced. In March 1990 the Liberal Democrats gave unanimous approval to a non-withdrawable 'Citizen's Income' – so now both 'Citizen's Income' and 'Basic Income' refer to an unconditional and non-withdrawable income paid to every individual.

During this history, pamphlets and books have been written, journals have been published, the idea has been debated at conferences, and the idea has come and gone on political agendas (it was discussed at a Labour Party conference during the 1920s), sometimes climbing the public agenda and then falling back again, but always returning in a more vigorous fashion and with a greater variety of people in favour.

The reason for this persistence and occasional revitalised emergence is that a Citizen's Income becomes more and more relevant as the years go by. One day a country will implement the idea, and then the rest of us will follow.

## 98

# A Citizen's Income would express some traditional values

Moral values remain valuable currency in the market-place of political debate. One 'Victorian value' still powerful in British political discourse is that it is virtuous to earn enough to support one's family (although 'family' would now have a broader definition than the Victorians would have given it). If I had been writing a few years ago then I would have said that the idea that a family should be constituted by two parents of different genders would remain a British moral value, but I would have been wrong. Public opinion can sometimes change very fast, and social policy and moral values can change with it.

William Temple, Archbishop of Canterbury during the first half of the Second World War, had been at Balliol College, Oxford, at the same time as William Beveridge, and the 'principles' that Temple listed – the sacredness of personality; fellow-membership; the duty of service; the power of sacrifice – [13] and some more practical but similar 'standards' that emerged from a conference held in Oxford in 1937 – the abolition of extreme poverty; equal opportunity of education; the safeguarding of the family; a sense of vocation in daily work; the earth's resources as belonging to the whole human race – [14] might all have helped to shape the UK's Welfare State (a term possibly first coined by Temple) as it came to birth during the Second World War.

When there are difficult decisions to be made, it is useful to have a set of values to fall back on, because it can be onerous to have to return to first principles all the time. Values that have stood the test of time can be a good place to start, but, as society changes, flexibility is also required, so for a society consciously to revisit its moral values is an essential process.

A Citizen's Income fits more closely with Temple's and the 1937 conference's values than with the 'Victorian' values with which I began. But a Citizen's Income also coheres with some 'Victorian' elements – such as the encouragement to make a contribution to society – so a Citizen's Income could be a useful way of creating links between the different sets of values that have informed our social policy during the last century or so. And if we had a Citizen's Income then we might find reasserting itself another value that has come and gone over time: universalism.

## 99

# A Citizen's Income would deliver a new kind of society

I have indicated some of the ideas and new social structures with which a Citizen's Income would fit, but does the combination of them add up to a coherent vision of a new society? Or is it just more patching, such as we have seen during the last century?

In the UK, Beveridge, Bevan and Butler, members of different political parties, created legislation on social security, health, and education, which created a coherent 'Welfare State'. It was felt to be coherent partly because such words as 'reconstruction' and such 'principles' as those enunciated by William Temple – the sacredness of personality; fellow-membership; the duty of service – were shared values in a fairly monochrome culture. The problem now is that we find it difficult to agree on a set of principles on which to base our social projects. Alasdair MacIntyre has suggested in his book *After Virtue* [15] that we have abandoned primary virtues and are left with such secondary virtues as fairness and cooperation. I am not so sure that we can distinguish between primary and secondary virtues in this way, but MacIntyre is right about our difficulty over agreed values.

So can we any longer hope to create what we would all agree to be a 'good society'? Yes, perhaps, if we can find some focus that is not a contested value. Perhaps 'unconditional gift' could function as the kind of total attitude that we might need, and as the focus for the kind of social project that our plural society will need as it changes ever faster. One gift-shaped experiment that we could try, of course, would be a Citizen's Income.

On one view a Citizen's Income is simply an administrative rearrangement, but on another view it would be a signpost to a very different kind of society, a society in which universality and unconditionality would be the primary characteristics. Such a society might seem a foolish project, but the arguments contained in this book suggest that it would not be at all foolish to place a gift-shaped social policy at the centre of our economic activity. A Citizen's Income might in fact be essential to our economy and our society in this still quite new millennium, because it might be one of the few ways available to us to fashion the kind of flexible economy and society that we are going to need. The fact that it would deliver a gift-shaped way of living would be a wonderful bonus.

# 100

## A Citizen's Income would be a bridge-builder

One of a Citizen's Income's important functions might be to build bridges between the diverse ideological commitments with which we will have to live in our increasingly plural society. During the Second World War, 'social insurance' fulfilled a similar function by linking liberal ideas about individual responsibility with a socialist commitment to collective provision.

A Citizen's Income would offer new social possibilities, but it might also serve a growing individualism. There is nothing wrong with this combination, providing that a Citizen's Income can bridge and to some extent reconcile such conflicting trends. It can; and a Citizen's Income would therefore enable us to manage transitions between different kinds of society with less disruption than we might experience with our current benefits systems.

Not only might a Citizen's Income build bridges between different kinds of society, but it might also create links between the most basic ideas that affect our social policy. A Citizen's Income would enhance the solidarity that we require if we are to reconcile liberty and equality; and we might also find that it can reconcile the pursuit of individual wealth with the pursuit of wealth for the community: because by springing the poverty and unemployment traps it would encourage both individual initiative and collaborative activity, would extend the tax base, and would create new wealth to be distributed as a larger Citizen's Income or to be used to create other public goods. Similarly, a Citizen's Income could make justice and efficiency compatible, as well as equality and diversity – and not simply compatible, but also mutually reinforcing.

We are not going to be short of social aims or ideologies in this new millennium. We might end up with too many of them. What matters is that they should get on with each other, at the practical as well as at the theoretical level. To reconcile concepts with one another is easy enough: the difficult bit is to create social policy that will act as a bridge between different ideologies, for if we cannot manage to do that then social policy will either oscillate as one ideology gives way to another, or it will stagnate out of fear of transgressing one ideology or another as it attempts to satisfy a more and more diverse electorate.

A Citizen's Income has the potential to bridge ideologies and to bridge different visions of society, so it is just the kind of social policy that we are going to need to enable a plural society to become progressively more plural and yet not disintegrate.

# In the cause of balance: nine and a half reasons for not establishing a Citizen's Income

### i There are problems that a Citizen's Income would not solve, such as the housing crisis

A Citizen's Income would not solve the housing crises that many cities in many countries are now suffering. A combination of planning regulations, restricted public revenues, international buyers seeing residential property as an investment opportunity, and expanding urban populations are making it difficult for housing supply to keep up with the demand for housing in many of our cities. Where means-tested housing benefits are in place their budgets are becoming unsustainable because the shortage of supply means that landlords can raise rents.

It is true that a Citizen's Income would not solve these problems. No benefits system can solve these problems. It is therefore not a problem that a Citizen's Income would not solve these problems.

But having said that, because a Citizen's Income would leave the economies of scale generated by people living together with the people living together – rather than extracting them for the Government, as means-tested benefits do – people would be more likely to form couples, and to live together in larger households; and because a Citizen's Income would take lots of households off means-tested benefits, so that no longer would their benefits rise if their rent went up, there would be less incentive for landlords to increase rents. So although a Citizen's Income would not solve the housing crisis, it would help to solve it, and it certainly wouldn't make it any worse.

The same might be true of the other problems that a Citizen's Income would not solve.

## ii   If a Citizen's Income were to replace means-tested benefits then we would not know who would be entitled to other benefits currently given to people on means-tested benefits

The UK now gives free school meals to all children in the first three years of schooling, but, beyond the age of seven, entitlement to free school meals is restricted to children whose parents are on means-tested benefits. Similarly, prescriptions are free to people on means-tested benefits. And because free school meals for over sevens act as a proxy for the level of poverty in a school population, the number of free school meals is a factor in calculating school budgets. If a Citizen's Income were to take lots of families off means-tested benefits then they and their schools would lose these associated benefits.

The answer is to grant free school meals to every child, to make everyone pay for prescriptions and reduce their cost, and for school funding to employ such educationally relevant criteria as the number of children without English as their first language.

## iii   A Citizen's Income would give scarce public money to people who do not need it

Public money is in short supply, so why give it to wealthy people who don't need it?

At first sight it does sound ridiculous to give money to people who are already wealthy. But once we recognise the administrative efficiency of doing so, the fact that giving money to everyone would mean that no stigma would attach to money given to the poor, the vital fact that to give money to everyone would not impose the marginal deduction rates that means-tested benefits impose, and the fact that the wealthy pay more in tax than they would receive in their Citizen's Incomes, and that their Citizen's Income would in any case simply replace their personal tax allowance, this reason for not paying a Citizen's Income to every citizen dissolves completely.

## iv   A Citizen's Income would not function as an automatic stabiliser during a recession in the same way that means-tested benefits do

During a recession, unemployment rises, people who lose their jobs receive unemployment benefit (whether contributory or means tested), and public money is thereby pumped into the economy, which is what the economy needs during a recession. A Citizen's Income would always be paid, so it would not have this effect.

The difference would in fact be rather less significant than it might look. Today, if someone loses their job, then the Government will cease to collect income tax from them (and other such taxes as the UK's National Insurance Contributions), and contributory or means-tested benefits will be paid out. The total increase in public expenditure is really the tax lost plus the benefits paid. If a Citizen's Income were to be paid by reducing personal tax allowances, then if someone with a Citizen's Income were to lose their job, the Government would suffer a larger loss of tax revenue and, if a Citizen's Income was not enough to live on, a certain amount of means-tested or contributory Unemployment Benefit would still need to be paid. The total of tax revenue lost plus additional benefits paid would be very similar to the total of tax revenue lost plus benefits paid out in today's context. The tax and benefits system, when looked as a whole system, would continue to function as an economic stabiliser during a recession.

If we had a Citizen's Income in place, then a future government would be able to achieve quantitative easing by adding additional sums to people's Citizen's Incomes for limited periods. The new money would then be more likely to be spent into the productive economy than is the kind of quantitative easing that bids up the price of government bonds and therefore benefits the already wealthy. To achieve quantitative easing through the Citizen's Income would benefit everyone.

## v A Citizen's Income designed for people who can earn incomes would not be sufficient for people with disabilities who cannot do so

A Citizen's Income would pay the same to everybody of the same age. People with disabilities experience costs higher than those of other people, and they are less able to seek employment. If a Citizen's Income were to replace means-tested and other benefits, then people with disabilities would not have enough to live on.

The answer to this objection is twofold. Most countries already have separate benefits for people with disabilities. Such benefits would be reduced to take into account the fact that people with disabilities, along with everybody else, would be receiving a Citizen's Income: but there is no reason for them not to continue. And if means-tested benefits with additions for people with disabilities were left in place, with a household's Citizen's Income taken into account in the same way as other income when entitlement to means-tested benefits was calculated, then people with disabilities would see a deduction in their means-tested benefits to match the Citizen's Income that they were now receiving. They would be no worse off.

What would not be possible would be higher Citizen's Incomes for people with disabilities or chronic illnesses. A major advantage of a

Citizen's Income is the ease of administration that would be delivered by its universality and unconditionality. The only variation would be in relation to the recipient's age: a variable that the recipient cannot control, and that would be easy to automate. The same would not be true for people with disabilities. This is why we would need to keep the current benefits for people with disabilities and then take their Citizen's Income into account when those benefits were calculated. Because the Citizen's Income would be so cheap to administer, it would be no problem to run it alongside the current mixture of local authority provision and means-tested benefits. Then we would be able to watch means-tested provision wither as claimants sought occasional appropriate employment to top up their Citizen's Incomes and disability benefits until only those unable to work at all were left on means-tested benefits.

### vi    A Citizen's Income would cause people to stop seeking paid work

The most important reason for not implementing a Citizen's Income, and the only one that does not dissolve completely on examination, is that we do not know what all of the effects of implementing a Citizen's Income would be. A significant effect might be people leaving the employment market.

Citizen's Income pilot projects in Namibia and India found that economic activity rose among people given a Citizen's Income, and particularly among women. This was because a foundational income gave to them the economic security to take risks and to start their own enterprises. Negative income tax experiments found that work effort changed little, but that people who became unemployed took longer to re-enter the employment market – probably because they were looking for the right job rather than for any job – and that employees with children would sometimes spend longer out of the employment market. Neither of these tendencies should be cause for regret. The evidence therefore suggests that a Citizen's Income would either increase economic activity, or would reduce it slightly in ways that might be helpful.

As for other unforeseen effects: we cannot foresee all of the effects of implementing a Citizen's Income, which is a reason for taking implementation slowly, either by starting with a small Citizen's Income and letting it grow, or by tackling one age group at a time. If a Citizen's Income were to replace personal tax allowances and proportions of means-tested benefits, then we would in any case be looking at a fairly small Citizen's Income. Tackling one age group at a time could be a good idea anyway, not least because public acceptability might depend on providing a Citizen's Income to those groups generally thought to be 'deserving' first before moving on to those containing people thought not so deserving.

## vii    A Citizen's Income would be unaffordable

Would tax rates have to rise beyond what people would accept? So is the idea a non-starter?

There are Citizen's Income schemes that would be unaffordable. A high Citizen's Income paid without reducing tax allowances or other benefits would not be affordable; and if a Citizen's Income were to be paid for by reducing personal tax allowances to zero and imposing the same income tax rate on everyone earning an income [1] then that single rate might be too high for low earners to manage. But there are also Citizen's Income schemes that would be perfectly affordable. The Citizen's Income Trust's scheme – which pegs Citizen's Income rates to the rates at which the UK pays out-of-work means-tested benefits, reduces personal tax allowances to zero, abolishes or reduces most means-tested benefits, and restricts tax relief on pension contributions to the basic rate – would be revenue neutral; that is, no additional public funding would be required. [2] A similar scheme with lower Citizen's Income rates, and that leaves in place means-tested benefits and takes a household's Citizen's Incomes into account when their means-tested benefits are calculated, is equally revenue neutral. [3] Even a scheme based on higher Citizen's Income rates pegged to the Minimum Income Standards calculated for the Joseph Rowntree Foundation [4] would require an average Income Tax rate (including National Insurance Contributions) of only 45%. If the tax system was sufficiently progressive, then the tax rates for lower earners could be quite manageable.

The objection will apply to some Citizen's Income schemes, but not to others. In relation to revenue neutral schemes, there can be no objection in relation to affordability.

## viii    Benefits systems are so complicated that it isn't possible to change them

Benefits systems tend to be quite complicated. The reason for this is that they have usually evolved during a long period of time. Changes have been made in response to problems that have arisen, usually without asking whether the structure of the system needs to be changed. So the structure remains the same and changes are made to the regulations, which then create anomalies elsewhere in the system, so additional changes are made – and so on. Once a system has reached a certain degree of complexity it really does look as if the only changes possible are minor ones in response to presenting problems; so the task of reviewing the structure as a whole looks ever more daunting. The UK's recent experience of trying to change the benefits system is not exactly encouraging. The Secretary of State, Iain Duncan Smith, is a brave man. He is attempting to roll several means-tested benefits into a single means-tested benefit, and at the same time implement a computerised delivery system that needs to operate flawlessly if the new benefit is going to work efficiently. The new Universal Credit is best seen as a mammoth changing of multiple sets of regulations. It is not a change in the structure of the system.

Every country's complexities are different, but every country has them. For instance, continental countries tend to have systems with functions shared between employers, trades unions, and the State; and the United States has different means-tested systems in each state. The systems that have evolved in developing countries are often different from those of developed countries (they tend to rely more on subsidising products than on contributing to household incomes), but they have their own complexities.

Because of all of this complexity, many potential benefits system changes would indeed be difficult to achieve – because they would themselves be complicated, and they would generate additional complexities within the existing benefits system. This would not be true of a Citizen's Income. A Citizen's Income is inherently simple, and so would not add to complexity. If the implementation of a Citizen's Income enabled parts of the existing system to be abolished, then simplicity would immediately be increased. If the existing system were to be retained, then many households would be able to leave behind the complex parts of the system, the Citizen's Income's effects would be entirely predictable, and the Citizen's Income would not add any additional complexity.

There is one change to benefits systems that will always be possible: a Citizen's Income.

## ix  People in employment would not be willing to fund a benefit that would be paid to surfers

Philippe Van Parijs raises the important question: would hard workers (the 'crazy') be willing to fund people who spend their lives surfing (the 'lazy')? [5]

Developed societies have already decided to fund payments to those not in paid work; and, on the whole, the people who pay for the benefits are not the people who receive them. A certain amount of resentment is understandable. And the way in which we pay benefits makes it difficult for people to get off them, so – if they understand what is happening – those who are paying for the benefits are paying for a system that ensures that people will continue to need them to keep paying.

A Citizen's Income would improve the situation in two respects. First of all, everyone would receive a Citizen's Income – including those doing the paying. And secondly, a Citizen's Income would enable people without sufficient other income to lift themselves out of any remaining means-tested provision.

As soon as they understood the effects of the transition to a Citizen's Income, taxpayers would be pleased.

## ix ½   There are other ways to lift people out of poverty

I call this final reason against a Citizen's Income half a reason because the answer is obviously 'yes': but that 'yes' is no reason not to implement a Citizen's Income, because the more ways we can find to lift people out of poverty the better.

A higher National Minimum Wage would contribute to lifting people out of poverty, and assuming that it was not set at a ridiculously high figure, any detrimental effects on the employment market would be negligible.

A job guarantee is sometimes suggested. This is not such a good idea, as it would skew the employment market and would require expensive supervision: but it could still help to lift out of poverty people living in areas in which a major employer had closed down.

A Citizen's Income could work alongside any other method of reducing poverty, and would itself contribute to lifting people out of poverty. The fact that other methods would help as well is welcome, but hardly relevant to the question as to whether a Citizen's Income would be useful – which it would be.

## 101

# A Citizen's Income is the system that we would choose

I shall state my final reason for a Citizen's Income in the form of a question that the reader might wish to answer after reading this book: if you were starting from scratch, would you invent the benefits systems that your country is now operating?

If we were starting from scratch (and it is a pity that we cannot do that), then would we not look at the reasons for a Citizen's Income, and at the reasons for the alternatives, and would we not choose a Citizen's Income as the foundation of our benefits system? If we did that, then we would fund it through a progressive income tax and other taxation, and we would then ask to what extent other social insurance and means-tested benefits might contribute to a thriving, plural and just society. If this is the process that we might follow in an ideal world, and it is possible to do the same in our non-ideal world, then should we not do it now?

# Notes

## A. ECONOMY

1   Richard Murphy and Howard Reed, *Financing the social state: Towards a full employment economy*, Centre for Labour and Social Studies, London, 2013, pp 25–7

2   Karl Widerquist and Allan Sheahen, 'The United States: The Basic Income Guarantee – past experience, current proposals', pp 11–32 in Matthew C. Murray and Carole Pateman, *Basic Income worldwide: Horizons of reform*, Palgrave Macmillan, New York, 2012, p 21

3   Guy Standing, *The precariat: The new dangerous class*, Bloomsbury, London, 2011; *A precariat charter*, Bloomsbury, London, 2014

4   According to the Office for National Statistics Labour Force Survey, in November 2014 there were approximately two million people unemployed. Approximately one million of these were in receipt of Jobseeker's Allowance. There were three unemployed people to every vacancy. www.ons.gov.uk/ons/rel/lms/labour-market-statistics/november-2014/dataset--claimant-count-and-vacancies.html

5   C.H. Douglas (an engineer), *Social credit*, Eyre and Spottiswood, London, 1933, pp 185–7; Keith Roberts (a scientist), *Automation, unemployment and the distribution of income*, European Centre for Work and Society, Maastricht, 1983; cf the politician and economist Jacques Duboin, *La Grande Relève des hommes par la Machine*, Éditions Fustier, Paris, 1932; *Égalité Economique*, Éditions Grasset, Paris, 1939; *Libération*, Éditions Ocia, Paris, 1946, pp 203–210; Jean-Paul Lambert (ed.), *Le Socialisme Distributiste: Jacques Duboin, 1878–1976*, L'Harmattan, Paris, 1998

6   For UK Minimum Income Standards, see www.jrf.org.uk/publications/minimum-income-standard-2014

7   Mike Danson, Paul Spicker, Robin McAlpine, Willie Sullivan, *The case for universalism: Assessing the evidence*, The Centre for Labour and Social Studies, London, 2014, pp 4, 11

8   R.H. Tawney, *Equality*, 5th edn, George Allen and Unwin, 1964 (first published in 1931), p 86

9   Ralf Dahrendorf, 'Can it happen?', an interview with Susan Raven, *BIRG Bulletin*, no.13, Citizen's Income Trust, London, August 1991, pp 12–13.

10  Thomas Piketty, *Capital in the twenty-first century*, Belknap Press, Cambridge, MA, 2014, p 353

[11] Pierre Teilhard de Chardin, *Le phénomène humain*, Éditions du Seuil, Paris, 1955; Thomas Kuhn, *The structure of scientific revolutions*, University of Chicago Press, Chicago, 1970; J.K. Galbraith, *Money: Whence it came, where it went*, Penguin, Harmondsworth, 1976


## B. A changing society

[1] Samuel Brittan and Steven Webb, *Beyond the welfare state: An examination of basic incomes in a market economy*, Aberdeen University Press, Aberdeen, 1990

[2] For example, New Zealand, Holland, and Denmark: Pensions Policy Institute for the National Association of Pension Funds, *Towards a Citizen's Pension*, National Association of Pension Funds, London, 2014, p.27: www.pensionspolicyinstitute.org.uk/publications/reports/towards-a-citizens-pension

[3] http://decorrespondent.nl/541/Why-we-should-give-free-money-to-everyone/20798745-cb9fbb39

[4] Pensions Policy Institute for the National Association of Pension Funds, *Towards a Citizen's Pension*, National Association of Pension Funds, London, 2014: www.pensionspolicyinstitute.org.uk/publications/reports/towards-a-citizens-pension

[5] Hartley Dean, The ethical deficit of the UK's proposed Universal Credit: pimping the precariat?' *Political Quarterly*, 83, 2, 2012, pp 353–9

[6] OECD Directorate on Employment Labour and Social Affairs, *Focus on inequality and growth*, OECD, Paris, 2014

[7] Bill Jordan, Simon James, Helen Kay and Marcus Redley, *Trapped in poverty? Labour-market decisions in low-income households*, Routledge, London, 1992, p 277

[8] B. Rothstein, *Is the universal welfare state a cause or an effect of social capital?*, QoG Working Paper Series, 2008:16: www.qog.pol.gu.se/digitalAssets/1350/1350669_2008_16_rothstein.pdf


## C. Administration

[1] From the Revenu Minimum D'Insertion (RMI), to the Revenu Minimum D'Activité (RMA), to the Contrat Unique D'Insertion – Contrat Initiative-Emploi (CUI-CIE).

[2] Department for Work and Pensions, *Family Resources Survey, 2012–13*, Department for Work and Pensions, London, 2014: www.gov.uk/government/collections/family-resources-survey--2:

[3] Sarath Davala, Renana Jhabvala, Soumya Kapoor Mehta and Guy Standing, *Basic income: A transformative policy for India*, Bloomsbury, London, 2014, p 38. The research team achieved bank accounts in 98% of households.

[4] Malcolm Torry, *Research note: A feasible way to implement a Citizen's Income*, Institute for Social and Economic Research, University of Essex, Colchester, 2014: www.iser.essex.ac.uk/research/publications/working-papers/euromod/em17-14

[5] James Meade, *Agathotopia: The economics of partnership*, David Hume Paper no.16, Aberdeen University Press, Aberdeen, 1989, pp 34–8. For a discussion of the evolution of Meade's ideas, see Tony Fitzpatrick, *Freedom and security: An introduction to the Basic Income debate*, Macmillan, Basingstoke, 1999, pp142–44

[6] Karl Widerquist and Michael W. Howard (eds) *Alaska's permanent fund dividend: Examining its suitability as a model*, Palgrave Macmillan, New York, 2012

[7] www.gov.uk/browse/benefits/entitlement

[8] www.community-links.org/uploads/documents/Secure_and_Ready.pdf

9    Mike Danson, Paul Spicker, Robin McAlpine, Willie Sullivan, *The case for universalism: Assessing the evidence*, The Centre for Labour and Social Studies, London, 2014, p 3

10   D.V.L. Smith and Associates, *Basic Income: A research report*, Prepared for Age Concern England, London, 1991, pp 5, 29

# Chapter 4

1    Alberto Nardelli, Ian Traynor and Leila Haddou, 'Revealed: Thousands of Britons on benefits across the EU', *The Guardian*, 19 January 2015: www.theguardian.com/uk-news/2015/jan/19/-sp-thousands-britons-claim-benefits-eu

2    www.flickr.com/photos/cabinetoffice/sets/72157647374093145/

3    William Beveridge, *Full employment in a free society*, Allen and Unwin, London, 1944

4    www.iser.essex.ac.uk/research/publications/working-papers/euromod/em17-14

5    Mike Danson, Paul Spicker, Robin McAlpine, Willie Sullivan, *The case for universalism: Assessing the evidence,* The Centre for Labour and Social Studies, London, 2014, p 21

6    Hansard, HC, 6th Series, vol. 191, col. 413, 16 May 1991

7    J.E. Meade, *The building of the New Europe: National diversity versus continental uniformity*, The Aberdeen University Press for the David Hume Institute, Aberdeen, 1991, pp 24–9

8    Malcolm Torry, *Research note: A feasible way to implement a Citizen's Income*, Institute for Social and Economic Research, University of Essex, Colchester, 2014: www.iser.essex.ac.uk/research/publications/working-papers/euromod/em17-14

9    Pensions Policy Institute for the National Association of Pension Funds, *Towards a Citizen's Pension*, National Association of Pension Funds, London, 2014, p 27: www.pensionspolicyinstitute.org.uk/publications/reports/towards-a-citizens-pension

10   www.commonwealthfund.org/publications/fund-reports/2014/jun/mirror-mirror

11   House of Commons Treasury and Civil Service Committee Sub-Committee, *The structure of personal income taxation and Income Support: Minutes of evidence*, HC 331–ix, Her Majesty's Stationery Office, London, 1982, p 459

# E. IDEAS

1    R.H. Tawney, *Equality*, 5th edn, George Allen and Unwin, 1964 (first published in 1931), p 86

2    Alex Cobham and Andy Sumner, *Putting the Gini back in the bottle? 'The Palma' as a policy-relevant measure of inequality*, King's College, London, 2013: www.kcl.ac.uk/aboutkings/worldwide/initiatives/global/intdev/people/Sumner/Cobham-Sumner-15March2013.pdf

3    OECD Directorate on Employment Labour and Social Affairs, *Focus on inequality and growth*, OECD, Paris, 2014

4    Mike Danson, Paul Spicker, Robin McAlpine, Willie Sullivan, *The case for universalism: Assessing the evidence*, The Centre for Labour and Social Studies, London, 2014, p 3

5    Ludwig Wittgenstein, *Philosophical Investigations*, 2nd edn, Basil Blackwell, Oxford, 1958, p 67

6    John Rawls, *A theory of justice*, Harvard University Press, Cambridge, MA, 1971, p 19

[7] Bill Jordan, *The common good: Citizenship, morality and self-interest*, Basil Blackwell, Oxford, 1989; Bill Jordan, 'Basic Income and the Common Good', pp 155–177 in Philippe Van Parijs (ed.) *Arguing for Basic Income: Ethical foundations for a radical reform*, Verso, London, 1992

[8] Ruth Lister, *Poverty*, Polity Press, Cambridge, 2004, pp 94-7, 145–6, 178–83

[9] John Hills, *Good times, bad times: The welfare myth of them and us*, Policy Press, Bristol, 2014

[10] Immanuel Kant, *Groundwork for the metaphysics of morals*, translated by Arnulf Zweig, Oxford University Press, Oxford, 2002 (first published in German in1785), pp 202–203

[11] Hamid Tabatabai, 'Iran: a bumpy road toward Basic Income', pp 285–300 in Richard Caputo (ed.) *Basic Income Guarantee and politics: International experiences and perspectives on the viability of income guarantee*, Palgrave Macmillan, New York, 2012

[12] James Meade, *Agathotopia: The economics of partnership*, David Hume Paper no.16, Aberdeen University Press, Aberdeen, 1989, pp 34–8

[13] William Temple, *Christianity and social order*, Shepheard-Walwyn/ SPCK, London, 1976 (first published in 1942)

[14] J.H. Oldham (ed.), *The churches survey their task: The report of the conference at Oxford, July 1937, on church, community and state*, George Allen and Unwin, London, 1937, p 108

[15] Alasdair MacIntyre, *After virtue: A study in moral theory*, Duckworth, London, 1985

## In the cause of balance: nine and a half reasons for not establishing a Citizen's Income

[1] A.B. Atkinson, *Public economics in Action: The Basic Income/ Flat Tax proposal*, Clarendon Press, Oxford, 1995, pp 24–46

[2] www.citizensincome/filelibrary/booklet2013.pdf

[3] www.iser.essex.ac.uk/research/publications/working-papers/euromod/em17-14

[4] www.jrf.org.uk/publications/minimum-income-standard-2014

[5] Philippe Van Parijs, *Real freedom for all: What (if anything) can justify capitalism?* Clarendon Press, Oxford, 1995, pp 89, 96